SANTA ABELLA
AND OTHER STORIES

Ken Wetherington

Santa Abella and Other Stories

Text © Ken Wetherington, 2020
Edward Street Books

Cover by BEAUTeBOOK, 2020
Original photography by Victoria Novillo Saravia

ISBN 978-0-578-69142-8

Also available in eBook.

The following have been previously published.

"Starstruck"
Bookends Review, June 2019

"Black Bear Lake"
Ginosko Literary Journal, Summer 2017

"One Night in Las Vegas"
Ragazine, January-February 2018

"Lydia"
Founder's Favourites, June 2019

"Between Eleven and Midnight"
Remington Review, Fall 2018

"Waiting for Adonis"
Remington Review, Spring 2019

"Thanatopsis"
The Fable Online, September 2017

For Valerie, my true love.

Special thanks go to Phillip M. Locey, Laurie Boris, Pete Barber, Richard H. Smith, Maria Novillo Saravia, all members (past and present) of my writing groups, and the many others who have encouraged and supported me along the way, too many to list here. I couldn't have done it without them.

Table of Contents

Santa Abella

I saw the knife plunge deep into his neck, but I never saw the blood. Too quickly, the crowd brushed me aside and swept him away into the night. I stumbled and careened into the path of a sweaty, obscenely corpulent brute. Lurching drunkenly, he shoved me to the ground, stepped heavily on my calf, and without pause barged through the multitude, a red bandanna around his neck and a patriotic fever in his eyes. By the time I struggled to my feet, I was lost in the turmoil of discontent.

I elbowed my way to the edge of the square and sought shelter in a doorway. The fighting flared and sputtered, illuminated here and there in the dimness of a few ancient streetlamps. The roar of the crowd surged and ebbed like an animal gasping for breath. A pair of teenage boys shouted as they ran past. Another youth hurled a bottle. It shattered against the door jamb, scattering a layer of glassy shrapnel on my head and shoulders.

Eventually, the mob roiled down the street for some unknown destination, leaving the square empty except for an old dog warily scavenging for food. I sank down, leaned against the doorframe, and closed my eyes.

When I awoke, the first light of dawn was edging into the eastern sky. A quiet stillness hung heavily in the morning air. I stretched my aching body and shook remnants of the glassy slivers from my hair.

The bruise on my right calf gave me an impressive limp. Pushing aside my own discomfort, I reluctantly assumed the responsibility to inform Dr. Gómez of the death of his friend.

I cut through the alley to Calle Trevino. Graffiti-covered walls expressed the sentiments, both mundane and profound, of the powerless. Last night's addition, *Viva El Tigre*, dominated the grimy canvas in large red letters.

Dr. Gómez resided in a two-story brick house a half-dozen blocks from the hospital. Many of his patients were high-level government officials with offices nearby. An eight-foot brick wall and an iron gate protected his privacy.

I rang the bell at the gate. A few minutes later, Juanita, his housekeeper, trundled out in a worn bathrobe. She recognized me immediately despite my disheveled appearance.

"El doctor no está aquí," she said sleepily through the bars of the gate.

"Not here? Do you know where he is?"

"Él se fue antes del amanecer."

"Did he have an emergency?"

"No sé. Probablemente."

"Do you know when he'll be back?"

"No, señor Maitland."

She took a step backwards. When I didn't speak, she turned, went inside, and no doubt back to bed.

I admired Dr. Gómez for the way he maintained his friendship with the dissident El Tigre while serving as physician to the power elite in the capital, his preeminent reputation providing a certain degree of immunity. Besides, everyone knew he grew up with El Tigre in a small town to the south. I assumed Dr.

Gómez had learned of El Tigre's injury and rushed to treat him. It would be a lost cause. With a deep neck wound, his friend would have bled to death in a matter of minutes.

My weariness had begun to take its toll. I limped back toward the Alfonso. By the time I reached the hotel, the sun had risen. Through the glass panels of the lobby, I observed the early risers beginning to stir. Norman Tragg's portly profile and thinning white hair were clearly visible as he conferred with two men unfamiliar to me.

I had been dodging former co-workers since quitting my job. Most of them shunned me in return, avoiding eye contact whenever I encountered them. They were still intent on playing the game and jockeying for position in the corporate structure. For me, it had become a tiresome endeavor. The actual work, if you could call it that, consisted of shuffling stacks of papers and tweaking numbers to justify official policies. In the final analysis, upper management decisions never seemed to mesh with real data or actual events, but their dictates were delivered with a certitude that forbade dissent.

I entered the hotel through the basement carpark. Héctor sat in the gatekeeper's booth, reading a newspaper. He looked up and stroked his small, neat moustache when I approached.

"Señor Maitland, you forgot your car." He flashed his jovial smile, probably hoping to receive a tip in return for some small service.

"No, Héctor. I've been out for a walk." He eyed my torn jacket and dirty shirt but held his tongue. "What's the news?" I asked.

"Not much, señor. You know this newspaper is

always a day or two behind the real news. I hear there was a riot last night."

I felt sure Héctor was a supporter of El Tigre but would never offer any opinion that might endanger a tip. I chose my words carefully.

"I think El Tigre may have been ... uh, injured in the riot." A troubled expression flickered across his face and then vanished. I wondered what he actually knew.

"No chance, señor. That cat still has nine lives."

"When I saw him, he was in bad shape. I don't think he's going to make it this time."

"No, no, señor. I hear he has escaped the capital and gone into hiding."

Héctor's ear was usually close to the ground in these situations. Could I have been mistaken? No, I was sure the knife had done its job, but I let the matter drop.

The elevator took me to the seventh floor. My room reminded me of all the things I wanted to ignore. Mounds of dirty clothes, stacks of newspapers, and unread books cluttered my living space. An old brief-case overflowed with obsolete reports, graphs, and other miscellany of my working life. Got to straighten up later, I told myself.

After showering and shaving, I thought of Julie. My wife had moved out about a year ago and immersed herself in local politics, becoming a crusader for reform and a fervent supporter of El Tigre. She answered every call—participating in voter registration drives, supporting striking workers in picket lines, and distributing leaflets on street corners.

The battery in my cell phone had expired, so I punched up her number on the landline. No answer.

I decided to get some breakfast and head over to the Trinidad where she was living.

Most of the early breakfast crowd had vacated the first-floor restaurant and moved on to their daily routine. From the buffet, I selected some lukewarm eggs, a couple of pieces of bacon, and a cup of coffee. No sooner had I taken a seat than I felt a presence behind me.

"Robert," said a voice at my elbow. It was Norman Tragg. "Haven't seen you around lately. Are you working for anyone now?"

"Between jobs, Norman," I grunted, hoping he would leave, but he sat down, coffee cup in hand.

"I thought you might have returned to Los Angeles. Just got back myself ... about a week ago."

"Yeah? How's the air back there these days?" I asked in my best mocking manner.

He shrugged, taking my question seriously. "Well, you know."

For a moment he stared at his coffee, stirring it absentmindedly. I had begun to think he had forgotten me.

"How's Julie?" he asked at last.

"Okay, I guess. I'm on my way over to the Trinidad. Thought I would check on her after the mess last night."

"Quite decent of you to do that. It's a shame you two split up. She's such a pretty girl. You should get back together. Well, give her my best." With that, he got up and left.

Julie would have bristled at being called a "girl," though "pretty" would have appealed to her vanity. She was an attractive woman but had a basic insecurity about her looks. That did not bode well for the time when the aging process would take its inevitable toll.

Out on the streets, the absence of traffic lent an unnatural quietness to the increasingly warm morning. Pedestrians hurried by on their way to work. The authorities had apparently issued a "do not drive" decree. That was the usual procedure during periods of unrest. In front of the Alfonso, a soldier dozed in the passenger seat of a military jeep while another leaned against the vehicle, smoking a cigarette.

It took only a few minutes to cover the half-dozen blocks to the Trinidad. Julie had the good sense to move to a less expensive room when we separated last year. I had been unable to summon the energy to do the same. I dabbed at the light sweat on my forehead with my handkerchief while I waited for the elevator, which never came. That was not a surprise. The facilities at the Trinidad were notoriously unpredictable.

I climbed the stairs to the third floor and rang her doorbell. After ringing a second time, I knocked but detected no sounds from inside. I lingered in the deserted hallway, hoping to flag down a neighbor for some news. Julie, unlike me, always knew her neighbors. After a couple of minutes, I gave up and returned to the lobby.

I tapped the bell on the counter. Its ring produced a clerk who gazed at me with an air of bored indifference.

"I'm looking for the lady in 310. Do you know where she is?" The clerk returned a blank stare. "La mujer en trescientos diez."

"No sé, señor."

"She hasn't checked out, has she? ¿Dejó el hotel?"

"No, señor."

"Have you seen her lately? I mean, uh … is she okay? She hasn't been ill or anything, has she? Uh … ¿enferma?"

"No sé, señor."

I muttered under my breath. It was doubtful the clerk's salary provided enough motivation to remember the hotel's guests. I left a note on a sheet of hotel stationery asking Julie to call me and then spent the rest of the morning wandering around the city. Soldiers loitered about in twos and threes. Beyond putting in an appearance, they seemed to have no specific duties.

After lunch at a cheap café, I returned to the Alfonso, the burrito weighing heavily on my stomach. At the front desk, I collected my mail and messages, which I had been neglecting for several weeks, and retreated to my room for a siesta. I got up around three o'clock and sorted through the bills and advertisements. Near the bottom of the stack, I came across a note, dated ten days ago, from Julie.

Bobby, I've gone to Santa Abella for a couple of weeks. I'll give you a call when I get back. — Julie

Though we led separate lives, some affection still existed between us. No, not affection really, but a connection. Neither of us desired to get back together nor wished to make an enemy of the other. An awkward, sporadic friendship ensued.

Santa Abella. That sounded vaguely familiar. I unearthed a map and located the tiny dot about a day's drive south of the capital. Then it came to me. El Tigre had been born there. He spent his childhood in Santa Abella before arriving in the capital as a young man.

Julie's nature drove her to seek out shrines of various sorts. She felt compelled to visit birthplaces and grave sites of the crusaders she admired. Once, she dragged me to a small village an hour's drive from the capital to see a marketplace where El Tigre had delivered a speech, advocating for increased agricultural subsidies. She delighted in soaking up a spiritual connection to the place. All I saw was a dusty, impoverished community trying to scratch out a living under miserable circumstances. We found no one there who remembered El Tigre's speech.

It didn't surprise me that she would make a pilgrimage to Santa Abella even if there was nothing to see. Later, she would likely mention it in conversation as if to authenticate her commitment to the cause. Well, that was that. She would return in a few days, regretting she missed the riot last night.

I put her out of my mind and went down to the carpark. My aging Ford had been sitting for a nearly a month and could use a spin about town to charge up the battery. Héctor still occupied the booth. A popular song crackled from his radio.

"Buenos días, señor Maitland."

"Buenos días, Héctor. I think I'll go for a drive."

"I'm sorry to tell you, but the policía have forbid all traffic."

"That's too bad, Héctor. Maybe tomorrow the ban will be lifted."

"Sí, mañana. I hope so. I would like to get my son to la casa de mi hermana en San Miguel for school."

"San Miguel, that's a pretty quick drive."

"Sí, but the bus it makes many stops and detours. It takes a day and a half if you have good fortune but most likely two days."

"Héctor, how would you like for me to run your son down to San Miguel as soon as this ban is lifted? I was thinking about going to Santa Abella, and it's right on my way." It wasn't true. I hadn't been planning the trip, but I saw an opportunity to break out of my rut.

Héctor's furrowed brow betrayed a trace of worry. He shook his head, his jet-black hair brushing his eyebrows. A moment of uneasy silence followed until I broke the spell.

"It's okay. If you'd rather send him on the bus ..."

"No, señor. It's just that I cannot afford to pay you, and the bus is very cheap."

I gave a little laugh. "Don't worry. It's on me. As I said, I was going anyway when the ban is lifted."

Héctor leaned close and whispered. "The ban will be lifted at midnight." I had no doubt Héctor knew in advance of an official announcement.

"Then it's settled. I'll stop by tomorrow morning and get your son. Emilio, isn't that right?"

Héctor beamed at my remembering his son's name. "Señor Maitland, you should leave at dawn if you want to make Santa Abella by nightfall. The roads are not so good after dark."

I groaned at the prospect of rising early. "Okay. I'll be here at eight o'clock." A flicker of concern clouded his features. "All right, seven-thirty."

He smiled. I didn't see how an extra half hour would matter much, though it seemed to make a difference to him. I returned to my room, packed my suitcase, and made a trip to the bank to withdraw a small portion of my diminishing funds. That evening I ordered a bland room service dinner to avoid seeing anyone. Afterwards, I watched a lousy "cops and robbers" movie on TV while consuming a couple of rounds of whiskey. I was ready for bed early.

I made it down to the carpark by a quarter of eight. Héctor's expression managed to convey both disapproval and relief. Emilio stood close by his side with a small, worn suitcase. He was a slight boy, about eight or nine years old, with his father's dark hair. He peered at me with apprehension. We passed the time in silence while Héctor retrieved my car.

The traffic ban had indeed been lifted, but few cars were on the streets. We crossed the Río Alvarez on a ramshackle bridge sorely in need of an upgrade. Once we were out of the city, an endlessly flat landscape emerged, broken only by a few knotty trees and an occasional cactus. The solar glare drove me to fish a pair of sunglasses from the glove box. They were so badly scratched the scenery resembled an old movie in soft focus. Still, they were better than nothing.

Emilio remained passive and silent until I turned on the radio. Then he immediately assumed control of the dial without asking, tuned it to his favorite station, and hummed drowsily to the popular songs. After he fell asleep, I switched it off.

Emilio's presence beside me stirred a memory of Julie. In the beginning, she had wanted children, and it had been my reluctance that delayed parenthood. Later, when she began to devote her energy to various causes, I thought a child might bring us closer together. By that time, our relationship had begun to fracture, and Julie wisely dismissed the idea. Her "work" had become too important.

I glanced at Emilio. For the first time in years, I contemplated the awesome responsibility a family brings. How difficult it must be for Héctor, on his small salary, to provide the necessities. I resolved to be more generous with tips for him. That is, as soon as I got my life and finances back on track.

By noon I was getting hungry. As if in answer to my stomach, a small dot appeared on the horizon and grew into a one-room adobe structure. The sign read "José's Gas y Burritos." An obese woman in heavy makeup and a red dress with white polka dots sat on a bench by the front door, cooling herself with a cardboard fan. I couldn't decide if she was a prostitute, or the wife of the proprietor, or both. I pulled up to the gas pump.

Emilio awoke with a yawn and a stretch. After topping off the tank, we went inside. José turned out to be a heavyset man in coveralls with the name "Fernando" stitched on the pocket. I selected two black bean burritos from a cooler and heated them in the microwave on the counter.

The dining accommodations consisted of two tables and three chairs. A couple of aisles of canned food took up most of the space. Emilio and I sat and ate our burritos with a soft drink for him and a beer for me. The burrito tasted like cardboard, but it sated my hunger, and Emilio didn't appear to mind. Soon, we were back on the road. Emilio found a soccer match on the radio and listened until it faded away.

"Do you like fútbol?" I asked, hoping for some conversation to pass the time.

"Sí, señor," he answered shyly.

"Do you play?"

"Sí, un poco."

"With your amigos?"

"Sí."

"Which is your favorite team?"

"Los Toros."

"How are they doing this year?"

"Son en el primer lugar."

"Do you have a favorite player?"

"Andújar. Él es un gran jugador."

It seemed more like an interrogation than a conversation, so I let it drop. Emilio appeared content to search for radio stations. I wondered why Héctor was sending him to San Miguel. The schools in the capital surely offered a more modern education than those of a small town. However, it was not my affair. I put the matter out of my mind.

The monotony of the drive, coupled with the beer, made me a little drowsy, though it wouldn't have mattered much if I meandered off the road. The hard plains of the desert were nearly as good for driving, but I held on course, thinking of Emilio in the seat next to me. By midafternoon, the tiny village of San Miguel came into view.

The red brick post office stood out as the only modern structure in town. It was a relief to find Emilio's aunt waiting as Héctor had promised. I half expected to have to go searching for her. She showered me with effusive thanks and offered a small payment, which I politely refused. With some effort, I escaped her hospitality, saying I had to get to Santa Abella before nightfall.

The last few hours of my trek stretched out interminably. The blazing reflection of the sun on the desert floor made driving difficult. I tried the sunglasses again. They provided only a minor improvement until the sun slid into the west, and its glare lessened. Twilight had begun to darken the sky as I pulled into Santa Abella.

To call it a town, or even a village, would be an overstatement. Only a handful of structures were evident. A two-story stone building housed the town hall and post office on the first floor. The second floor served as a hotel. A saloon and a gas station faced each other across the main drag. The scene was bracketed by a church at one end and at the other, a cemetery, enclosed by a leaning, wooden fence. I saw no houses or farms. I wondered where the locals lived if one could call this living.

The town hall and post office were closed. I made my way upstairs to the hotel where an attendant slept at his small desk in the hallway. I woke him, and he handed me a room key.

"¿Cuánto cuesta?" I asked.

He contorted his face in an attempt to stifle a yawn. "Mañana."

The tiny room held a single bed, a small table, and a mirror. I would have to live out of my suitcase. The bathroom was down the hall. My weariness overcame the thin, unyielding mattress, and I slept.

In the morning, last night's clerk had been replaced by a heavyset woman. She eyed me with suspicion but accepted my money without question. Downstairs, neither the town hall nor post office had opened. I wandered out into the street.

At the service station, a farmer pumped gas into the tank of his battered truck. I strolled over to check out the adobe structure, its whitewashed surface marked by years of exposure to the elements. Inside, an old man with a big, white moustache sat on a stool behind the cash register. A counter with coffee and doughnuts for sale occupied nearly half the tiny interior. Across the dirt floor on the opposite wall, a couple of shelves held a dozen dusty cans of motor oil. I tried the coffee, which was hot and tasteless. I passed on the stale-looking doughnuts and asked the attendant if he had seen an American woman recently, receiving only a vacant stare in response.

With no definite plan in mind, I decided to check out the church. The white, stone structure was old and small but projected a solidity that the other buildings did not. I entered and found a clean, austere interior. Its crude wooden pews were guaranteed to keep the flock awake even for the dullest of sermons. A short, raised stage held a pulpit in front of a surprisingly large painting of Mary and the baby Jesus.

Leaving the church, I saw two men with shovels digging in the cemetery. Just inside the gate, a half-dozen men wrestled two coffins from an old-fashioned hearse.

The post office finally opened for business. An elderly postal clerk, with a face full of wrinkles, sorted mail behind the counter. His bald head bobbed up and down as he flicked letters into cubicles. He looked up when I entered.

"¿Habla inglés?"

He turned and glanced over his shoulder toward the back of the room where a young man vigorously attacked a typewriter. "Luis!" he called. The young man raised his head, flashed a big smile, and approached the counter.

"Buenos días, señor."

"Buenos días. ¿Habla inglés?"

"Sí, señor."

"I'm looking for a blond American woman in her late twenties. She would have been here a week or two ago, but she hasn't returned to the capital."

14

"No, señor. I have not seen your lady."

"Are you sure? She's slender and kind of pretty."

"Like a supermodel, señor?"

I laughed, knowing the comparison would have appealed to Julie. "Not exactly. She's pretty though not the glamorous type. If you hear of anyone seeing her, let me know. I'm staying upstairs for a few days."

As I turned to leave, I heard Luis whispering to the old man. "Todos los Americanos estan buscando una muchacha linda." Muffled laughter followed.

Across the hall, a middle-aged woman was unlocking the town hall office. I lingered in the doorway. "Un momento," she said as she flipped on the light switch and began to organize her desk for the day's work. I stepped outside while she got settled.

Over at the cemetery, the gravediggers rested in the shade of a solitary tree. A tall man in a gray suit and a stocky figure in white stood over the new mounds of earth. A trio of small, ragged children looked on.

I briefly contemplated the mortality rate in Santa Abella. It must be high. Surely no quality medical facility existed between here and the capital. I pushed away a pang of guilt. Even with my dwindling funds, I could see a doctor anytime in the capital. Julie would have seized upon the twinge of guilt and built a cause from it or at least begun the fight until some other injustice took her attention.

When I returned to the town hall office, the clerk had coffee brewing and was fussing with an uncooperative typewriter. I wondered when computers would reach Santa Abella. Finally, she settled at her desk and glanced at me with raised eyebrows.

"Estoy buscando una muchacha linda," I said. Her

expression did not change. "Una Americana," I added.

"No Americanos en Santa Abella," she replied with an air of apathy. She picked up a folder and began to examine some forms.

"Hace una semana, tal vez dos."

"No Americanos en Santa Abella," she repeated without looking up.

I had come to a dead end. Maybe Julie never made it to Santa Abella. I considered the possibility her note was intended to mislead me. Perhaps she had gone off on an adventure with a new lover and didn't want to hurt my feelings. I rejected that notion. It wasn't like her to be deceitful. The note had been sincere enough, but her plans might have changed. It wouldn't necessarily have occurred to her to let me know.

Back out on the street, the sun had begun its daily baking of the landscape. The saloon was closed and probably would not open until evening. Desiring only to escape the heat, I returned to my hotel room with its inadequate air-conditioning.

Between dozing and sweating, the morning dragged by. Noon passed without triggering any desire for lunch. The uncomfortable bed made meaningful rest impossible, though getting up held no appeal either. By late afternoon, the sun had reached my side of the building. The rising temperature forced me from my malaise.

The attendant had vanished from the desk in the hallway. I suspected he or she was taking a siesta in one of the rooms. Outside, the shadows had begun to stretch across the street. I hoped there would be some activity at the saloon.

Inside the tiny, dark establishment, two tables and one booth sat awkwardly askew on the uneven dirt floor. The bartender, a small man with a sad face, sat on a stool in front of a cabinet, which presumably held the liquor. I had the place to myself. I wondered why since drinking was the only entertainment in sight.

My inquiries to the bartender were met with "No sé, señor." It was the response I expected. I didn't press him further. My desire to locate Julie had begun to wane. After downing a couple whiskeys, I made my way over to the church and took a seat on a small bench shaded by the steeple.

Occasionally, a local would wander into the saloon. Once, a car pulled up to the hotel-town hall-post office, a fairly recent model by Santa Abella's standards. The driver, with an envelope in hand, entered only to emerge a minute later and drive away.

I walked over to the cemetery. A rusty tin sign on the gate stated the obvious, *El Cemeterio de Santa Abella*. The few dozen sad-looking graves reeked of the poverty and despair endemic to life and death in this remote, miserable place. Several were adorned with wilted flowers. Even the most recent tombstones appeared ancient, bearing the scars of wind and sand. I turned my attention to the two new graves. One of them sported a vase of freshly cut roses, which looked remarkably fine, all things considered. I wondered how they had been cultivated in this climate. It was too soon for tombstones. Nice flowers and new tombstones would not matter. Before long, these latest graves would resemble the others, covered by the perpetual dust of Santa Abella.

The shadows began to lengthen, and the heat eased marginally. I sat on a rough bench by the gate and watched the afternoon fade to dusk, the dusk to twilight, and twilight to night. The saloon attracted four or five weary men. I envisioned them drinking in silence, each wrestling with his own demons. I resisted the temptation to have another drink, returning instead to the hotel. Getting to bed early and heading home in the morning seemed my best option.

The night clerk, upstairs at the hotel, waved me over and pushed an envelope toward me. It was addressed simply in a neat script, "Robert Maitland." I wondered who had managed to track me down.

In my room, I paused before opening it and ran my hand across its surface. The stationery was of high quality. I used my pocketknife as a letter opener, unfolded the single sheet, and read the few lines of typed text.

Señor Maitland,

I welcome you to our humble town of Santa Abella. Unfortunately, our local facilities are less than luxurious. Please grant me the honor of being my guest for dinner tomorrow evening. My driver will pick you up at six o'clock. Please dress casually. I am a friend of your wife and can answer some of your questions.

Cordially,
Eduardo Molina

I returned to the clerk in the hallway. "¿Quién es Eduardo Molina?"

"Es el agricultor con el rancho más grande."

"¿Dónde?"

"Oeste," he replied with a bored wave.

Who was this mysterious and wealthy farmer? I wondered how Julie knew him. Were they lovers? I didn't want to think about it.

* * *

The heat woke me early. I hadn't eaten since having the burrito with Emilio a day and a half ago. The gas station offered the same fare as yesterday. This time, I choked down a couple of stale doughnuts with the flavorless coffee. I asked the attendant where Eduardo Molina lived. He pointed through the small window in the back wall. All I saw were the distant mountains, probably farther away than they appeared. My puzzled reaction caused him to point again. I went to the window and squinted. A tiny strip of green near the base of the mountains caught my eye.

"¿Rancho?"

"Sí."

"¿Grande?"

"Es muy grande."

It turned out that he had never seen Molina but imagined him to be a man of fabulous wealth. If so, what he was doing in this godforsaken place? When the post office opened for business, I got much the same response to my inquiries. A little later, the woman in the town hall office warned me that Molina was quite the ladies' man and I should keep a close watch on my wife if I found her there, but like the others she had never laid eyes on him.

The afternoon stretched out before me with nothing to do until six o'clock, so I walked over to the church again. A young woman in a faded dress labored at sweeping the front steps. She was losing the battle, an endless task requiring either faith that the dust would eventually be banished or resignation to the eternal struggle. She stepped aside and smiled shyly as I entered.

The priest sat in one of the pews with his head bowed. Not wishing to disturb him, I turned to leave and banged my knee on a pew. It sounded louder than it should have. I eased into the back row, rubbing my knee and flexing my leg. The priest, a small man with a round face, approached quickly. He carried a wide-brimmed black hat.

"Are you injured, my son?"

"No, just a minor bruise, I think."

"Can I get you anything?"

"Your English is very good. No, I'm okay. I didn't mean to disturb you."

"I can pray anytime. It's not often I have an American visitor. Are you enjoying your stay in Santa Abella?"

"It's not a vacation, Father. I'm looking for someone."

"Your wife, they say."

"Have you seen her? She's a slender woman with light hair."

"No, she's not here in town."

"You've seen her somewhere?" I stood up.

"There was a young American woman at señor Molina's recently. I didn't see her, but I heard she was there."

"It must have been her. I have an invitation from señor Molina for dinner tonight."

He smiled. "I guess you've found her."

"I don't think so. The note said he had information."

"Perhaps he knows where she is."

"Possibly."

"I'm sure you will find señor Molina to be a helpful

man."

"What's he like? Pretty wealthy, I hear."

"Yes, he has a big house, large farm, and a helicopter, which takes him to the capital periodically."

"I didn't know about the helicopter, but what's he like personally?"

"He's a cultured man who sometimes likes to pretend he's a revolutionary. It's easy for the rich to pretend in that way, especially here in the birthplace of El Tigre. Some of the locals believe he's on their side, and he is, up to a point."

"You sound a little critical, Father."

"We all have our faults. Look at this." He gestured toward the large painting I had seen yesterday.

"It's very impressive," I said. He pointed to a small brass plate on the frame. I moved closer. It read, *Regalo de Eduardo Molina.* "Then it's a gift from him."

"It's a cultured gift. Possibly it inspires faith in a few of my flock, but food assistance or financial help would go further. These people are poor and many are hungry."

"And he gives no money to help the poor?"

"I wouldn't say that. He does give and quite generously, though some of his gifts, like this painting, don't have such a direct benefit to the parishioners."

Julie would be drawn to this man of mystery, contradictions, and revolutionary passions. I couldn't hope to compete with romantic figures like El Tigre and Molina. She would, no doubt, desire to engage in some grand conspiracy to advance the cause. Maybe she would be there tonight unless she had already returned to the capital. In either case, there was nothing for me to say to her. I considered ducking my invitation and returning to the city. If I left right away,

I would be back around midnight. I couldn't really say why I had come in the first place. The priest spoke, interrupting my thoughts.

"Speaking of hunger, may I offer you lunch? It won't be nearly as fancy as your dinner tonight. There's a small kitchen by my office, and Maria is making tortillas. By the way, my name is Juan Garza."

I started to decline, but my stomach reminded me I had eaten little since leaving the capital. We entered the tiny kitchen where a small table and three chairs were tucked into one of the corners.

While we ate, Father Garza told me of his childhood in Washington, DC, which accounted for his English. His father had worked for an international relief agency there. While a young man, he became fascinated with and then repelled by the Scientology church near their apartment. The hypocrisy he found among the government institutions added to his disillusionment. He came to the realization that many federal agencies, which professed to offer assistance to average citizens and small businesses, fell short of their mandates, often thwarted by their own bloated bureaucracies.

In frustration, Father Garza abandoned Washington and decided to work to make a difference by becoming a priest. His life hadn't turned out as planned, but he accepted his fate, which had led him to this remote spot and charged him with many destitute parishioners. I could see his intelligence, good humor, and dedication served him well.

When we finished our meal, I thanked Father Garza and returned to the hotel. My siesta was deep and long. I awoke with just enough time to bathe and dress before señor Molina's car arrived.

The driver, attired in a chauffeur's uniform, tugged at his collar, which seemed a little tight. I leaned forward as we pulled out of town.

"¿Habla inglés?"

"Sí señor. A little."

"How far to señor Molina's house?"

"Not far by auto. There, at the foot of the mountains."

I peered forward, holding my hand up against the glare of the sun. I failed to make out the strip of green I had seen earlier. "How long until we get there?"

"Una hora."

I peeked over his shoulder at the speedometer, which hovered around seventy. The ride over the hard, sandy plain was smooth. The comfortable distance between the driver and me made conversation an effort. I sat back and allowed myself to enjoy the opulent ease of the finely tuned automobile.

Soon, we were zipping by vast green fields supported by a massive irrigation system. I tapped the back of the front seat, and the driver turned halfway toward me.

"¿Dónde agua?" I gestured toward the fields.

"Las montañas, uh … the mountains, señor Maitland."

It must have been a costly project, though the local labor was probably cheap. A short while later, we pulled up to a large white mansion fronted by four columns. A well-tended lawn stretched out before it.

A formally dressed servant, waiting on the steps, steered me through the front door and into a spacious and impressively ornate foyer with a mammoth staircase. He led me to a large drawing room crowded with furniture and a grand piano. A few minutes later,

Molina, a tall man with shiny black hair combed flat, entered. He had a narrow moustache and exuded a genial air. His casual shirt and slacks looked expensive.

"Welcome to my home, señor Maitland."

"Thank you for inviting me, señor Molina."

"Please call me Eduardo."

"Robert," I replied with a nod.

A servant appeared with a bottle of brandy and two glasses. When we were seated with our drinks, Molina spoke.

"Robert, I know you have some questions about your wife, but first let's get to know each other over dinner. We have the whole evening ahead of us."

Perhaps he needed time to gauge my reaction to the news that he and Julie were lovers. He seemed a cautious man in that way despite his generally confident manner. If things went well, maybe Julie would join us after dinner.

He told me about his poor childhood, his determination to excel in school, and paying for college by working two jobs. He entered the banking business and made a fortune but found it dull. Next, he turned to farming, which he discovered to be gratifying and profitable. I related a brief summary of my less than successful life, mentioning that Julie and I had separated. He listened with sympathy. Around eight o'clock, the servant returned to announce dinner.

The surprisingly simple fare, chicken with rice and vegetables, was cooked to perfection and lightly seasoned with a spice I couldn't quite identify. The excellent Sauvignon Blanc perfectly complemented the meal.

My host regaled me with stories of the small

triumphs and tragedies of the locals and his sensitivity to their plight. After dinner, we retired to the drawing room with our wine glasses. I declined his offer of a cigar. He put the box away without taking one for himself. He settled into an overly stuffed armchair, and I sat on the matching sofa.

"Robert, I understand you are searching for your wife."

"Yes, though we're separated, as I told you. We've managed to remain friendly, more or less. I've been worried about her since things have been chaotic in the capital. She left a note saying she was coming to Santa Abella."

"Yes, she's been here, but I have some rather bad news." Molina paused and looked me in the eye. "Your wife became ill and passed away a few days ago."

"B-but how? What?" I stuttered, rubbing my forehead and trying to comprehend his words. Did he really mean Julie was dead? It couldn't be true.

He bent forward and repeated his statement, this time with more empathy. He reached out and touched me lightly on the knee.

He withdrew his hand and leaned back in his chair. "It was all very sudden. A fever. She lasted only a couple of days. Our local doctor was unable to help her. I doubt even the best medical treatment would have saved her."

Julie, gone. It felt like a dream or rather a nightmare. Reality receded, leaving me numb until my host spoke again and drew me back to the present.

"She was staying here," Molina continued. "I would have provided any medical care for her, but the doctor said she had no chance."

"Here …," I mumbled. "Were you lovers?" I hadn't

meant to ask so bluntly. The words seemed to come of their own accord. It took a moment for him to respond.

"No, Robert. She was interested in our local history, El Tigre especially. I invited her to stay here." He rose and put his hand on my shoulder. "I have another who is my mistress. She spends half her time in the capital. Santa Abella is not exciting enough for her. Your wife was a beautiful woman and very smart. You are a lucky man to have had some time together."

I wanted to ask why he had waited so long to tell me, but my mind worked slowly through the shock and alcohol. Did he feel the need to lull me into a semi-drunken state to break the news? Maybe boredom with the lack of social life in Santa Abella drove him to make a show of hospitality for another American guest. It was too much to process.

"May I speak to the doctor?"

"At present, he is making his rounds in the countryside. He'll be back in a week or so. There is no other local doctor. He covers hundreds of square miles in an old car, which frankly has seen better days. I should buy a new one for him. It's the least I could do in payment for his invaluable service to the citizens of Santa Abella. I shall speak to him about it upon his return."

"Where's Julie? Her uh ... body, I mean."

"She was laid to rest only yesterday in the local cemetery. The doctor thought it best for her to be buried quickly. He was unsure about the nature of the fever, and well ... as I said he thought it best. At the time, I did not know you were in town. Naturally, we would have notified you. My apologies for our haste. Her burial had barely been completed when I discovered you were here."

I remembered the gravediggers and realized I had seen her funeral, or rather her burial, on my first morning in Santa Abella. How sad that only strangers were there for her. I fought back the tears. Molina offered a handkerchief. I buried my face in it and struggled to regain my composure. Finally, I managed to gather myself.

"Thank you, señor Molina, for the evening," I mumbled, rising to my feet. "And the information."

"Eduardo please, Robert."

"Right, Eduardo."

"You are welcome to spend the night here. I can assure that you will be comfortable."

"No thanks. I want to get an early start tomorrow. It's a long, hot drive. I, uh … want to spend a little time at the cemetery."

"I understand. There's no gravestone. I can have one made."

"That's a generous offer, but it's too expensive."

"Robert, the cost is a small matter to me. After all, she was my guest. Should it say, 'Loving Wife' or something?"

"No, I guess not. I can't think of the right words."

He nodded and led me to the front door. His driver appeared and helped me into the car.

The comfort of the ride, the effects of the wine, and my weariness overcame me. The driver roused me when we reached Santa Abella. He offered to assist me to my room. I declined with a wave and grunt.

I awoke in the morning, still dressed from the previous day. After washing up and changing, I made my way down to the street. Shading my eyes, I glanced toward the cemetery. I wasn't quite ready to pay my last respects to Julie.

To my surprise, the saloon was open. Apparently, the business hours varied according to the whims of the proprietor. As before, the bartender with the sad face manned the bar. I ordered a whiskey and seated myself at a crude table. The rickety chair, made more precarious by the uneven dirt floor, was not very comfortable, but the windowless gloom appealed to me.

I had taken my first sip when another man entered. Sunlight poured through the open door, temporarily blinding me. The heavyset newcomer, dressed in a rumpled white suit, approached the bartender. When he had his drink, he turned and walked toward me. My eyes were still adjusting as he spoke.

"Hello, Robert. Fancy seeing you here."

I squinted. He came closer and seated himself at my table.

The graying hair, round eyeglasses, and droopy moustache were familiar though out of place. A moment later, I recognized him.

"Dr. G-Gómez," I stammered. "What are you doing here? I came to your house on the night of the riot. It was late. Actually, it was the following morning. I had been out all night."

"A night of brutality," he said grimly.

"El Tigre must be dead. I saw him stabbed. He couldn't have lived. Do you know what happened to him?"

"I know very little, Robert, mostly hearsay and rumor. I was away with an emergency, but you may be wrong about his death. If he's dead, his supporters would be making him into a martyr."

"Well, it was chaotic that night. I saw him only

briefly. I was certain ... Are you looking for him?"

"Not exactly, though I am worried. He may have been injured. I hoped his friends here might have some information."

"Do you mean Molina?"

"He's one, but El Tigre has many friends in Santa Abella. He was born here, you know."

"Yes. Uh ... Doctor ...?

"What is it, Robert?"

"Do you treat Molina when he's ill?"

"Heavens no! He has a doctor in the capital who charges much more than I do."

"Have you been to his place in the past few days?"

"No, I've been staying with friends. I'll pay him a visit before I leave."

"Doctor ... he told me Julie's dead."

"No! Really? I'm very sorry, Robert. What happened?"

I related my encounter with Molina while Dr. Gómez listened and sipped his drink. After a moment of silence, he spoke.

"I'm very sorry, Robert," he repeated. "There are fevers here that come on very quickly. Who knows why?"

"But Doctor, I, uh ..." I couldn't formulate a question. "It's all a shock. I can't wrap my mind around it."

"Perhaps you need to get back to the capital and into your routine. Are you working these days?"

"Some," I lied.

"Then that's my suggestion as a friend and a doctor. And Robert ..."

"Yes?"

"Try not to drink too much," he said, downing the remainder of his whiskey.

"Yeah, I guess you're right," I replied as I finished mine.

He shuffled to the door and out in a blaze of brilliant sunlight. I sat for a few minutes. Then it was time to pay my last respects to Julie.

The arid climate had already robbed the recent graves of their newness. Without markers I had no way to know which was hers. Yet, in an odd way, I felt closer to her than I had in a long time.

I seated myself on an old bench. My thoughts drifted back over my life with Julie. I reflected only on the good times and refused to allow the troubled moments to intrude. It was the least I could do. The afternoon slipped away. Later, as the sun sank toward the horizon, I returned to my room where I slept soundly.

Rising early, I paid my bill and headed back to the capital. I thought about Julie for a while, of the odd end she had come to, and of El Tigre and his uncertain fate. Eventually, my mind let it all go. I simply drove.

In those mindless hours, I discovered, through my scratchy sunglasses, a rare beauty in the barren landscape. The flatness of the plains, punctuated by the occasional scraggly tree or lonely cactus, lent a mood of serene melancholy to the drive. Even the dust cloud, which spread behind my car, sank gracefully to the desert floor as if retiring for the evening.

Darkness had fallen when I pulled into the carpark. The night man dozed in the gatekeeper's booth. I didn't disturb him. He would likely sleep until Héctor woke him in the morning. Back in my room, I showered to wash away the dust and relaxed with a whiskey before going to bed.

I rose at dawn, straightened my room, and took out

the trash. Halfway through packing, I paused to wonder where I was going. Dropping heavily on the sofa, I resisted the urge for a drink. Los Angeles, I thought. I must be going home. I called the airport and charged a ticket to my nearly maxed-out credit card. After snapping my suitcase closed, I surveyed the room. My remaining possessions lay scattered about. Nothing among them held any value for me. I called the front desk and charged the balance of the bill to my credit card, hoping it wouldn't exceed my limit.

I couldn't bring myself to exchange greetings with Héctor and answer his polite inquiries about my trip to Santa Abella, so I made for the lobby. Norman nodded to me as I passed through. I gave a quick wave, exited the front door, and got into the nearest cab.

The airport teemed with humanity. The recent unrest had sparked an exodus. Many of those leaving now would be back in a month or so. While I waited for my flight, I recalled life with Julie in LA.

Our marriage had started well, but her enthusiasm for social causes didn't mesh with my indifference. When the Latin American opportunity arose, I jumped at it in hopes of reviving our relationship. Once here, things got worse instead of better, and we separated. At least it had been a mutual decision. I could no longer say why we had embarked on a life together in the first place.

Two maintenance men, working nearby, interrupted my reverie as they speculated about El Tigre's fate. I eavesdropped. El Tigre was still missing or in hiding. They anticipated waves of euphoria among his followers when he re-emerged with a new and dynamic strategy. They were not yearning for a martyr. They were counting on a real, live champion.

I wished for a cause to compel me to some sort of action. Dimly, I heard my flight called. It felt like too much trouble to get up and go to the gate. Sometime later, I shuffled outside, looking for a cab to hail.

Starstruck

Vanessa Jackson slipped gracefully out of her clothes and frolicked across the sand. Her lithe body and flowing blond hair fed my long-held fantasies. She splashed into the shallow surf, and when the water reached her waist, she plunged beneath the waves. After a few seconds, her head bobbed up.

"Cut," yelled Morgan Breedlove. He gestured in my direction, and I snatched up a towel and robe and ran to meet Ms. Jackson as she emerged from the sea. I held up the robe for privacy while she dried herself.

She rewarded me with a smile. "Thank you, Angie." She slid one arm and then the other into the robe, knotted the sash, and linked her arm in mine as we trudged back to the camera set-up. "The water's damn chilly," she said, shivering. The scent of her body mixed with the saltiness of the ocean air made my head swim, and I stumbled.

"Whoa, girl," she said with a laugh. "Don't injure yourself. You're all I've got this weekend." I righted myself and nodded.

Morgan approached, smiling. "Nice, darling, but let's do one more. I want to see your joy, but don't flaunt it quite so much." He turned to his cameraman. "Take five, Christof. We'll get her dried off and have another go."

I collected her discarded clothes and followed her into the small changing tent. She handed me a battery-powered hair dryer and comb.

"Thanks for shielding me, Angie. Ouch, too hot."

I adjusted the dryer. "Sorry." I fluffed out her hair while the dryer hummed, hardly believing my fairy tale luck. If her personal assistant hadn't fallen ill ...

After a few minutes, she pushed the dryer away. "That's good enough, Angie. It doesn't have to be perfectly dry. There's no close-up to worry about." She stepped out of her robe and into her clothes. "Let's give the guys another chance to gawk." I must have looked shocked because she followed up. "Nude scenes are just business. This one's not so bad—only the three of you on the set. Anyway, half the time those scenes get cut to avoid the R rating, though I'll bet Morgan and other directors preserve the footage for their personal enjoyment. Come on. Let's get it done."

It took three additional takes before Morgan pronounced his satisfaction. Each time, I became bolder in stroking her hair. After the final take, I casually put my hand on her shoulder as I combed. Did she welcome it? She didn't object, but neither did she offer encouragement. My heart raced, and I struggled to stay outwardly calm. Did she notice? I couldn't tell. After all, acting was her profession. I wondered if her publicized romance with Lawrence Fuller, an up-and-coming young actor, was a fiction dreamed up by the tabloids.

We walked together back to the hotel, leaving Morgan and Christof fussing over some issue with the camera. Perhaps the scene would require re-shooting. I hoped so. Just before reaching the hotel, she turned to me.

"Make sure Morgan pays you. He forgets details sometimes."

"Yes, Ms. Jackson."

"Call me Vanessa."

"Thank you ... Vanessa. The money's not necessary. It's a wonderful experience."

"Don't be a fool. Always get paid."

She gave my arm a squeeze, and we went up to our rooms, which were adjoined by a connecting door. Morgan had impressed upon me that I should be ready to do her bidding on short notice. I tried to nap before dinner, but thoughts of her just beyond the door kept me on edge. My mind surged, recalling the unlikely circumstances that had brought me here.

* * *

The Literature Club at my high school had adjourned and everyone was gone, except for Alex Conley and me. He had been trying to impress me with his superior intellect for months.

"How about a movie this weekend?" he asked. "There's a documentary at the Chelsea."

I sighed. He made an acceptable partner for literary banter, but I had no desire to go out with him, so I lied. "Sorry, I've got a paper to finish."

He frowned and stuffed a book into his backpack. Before he could renew his request, Principal Boxer appeared in the doorway with a man I didn't know.

"Angie, I'd like a word with you."

Could I be in trouble? What had I done, and who was the stranger? The principal gave a dismissive glance at Alex, who zipped up his backpack and hastily departed, probably relieved he was not the object of attention.

"Angie, this is Eric Thorne. He graduated from here eight years ago. Now he's with Ambient Films. They're shooting a few scenes around town and at the beach this weekend."

I smiled. "Nice to meet you."

Eric looked me over with a gaze that left me slightly uncomfortable. "How old are you, Angie?"

"Seventeen. Eighteen, in three weeks. Birthday's the first of June." What did he want? Was he hunting for extras?

His phone buzzed. He gave it a quick check and then turned his attention back to me. "How would you like to make a little money this weekend?"

"Doing what?"

"One of our crew has fallen ill. We're a small operation and we need someone to run errands for our leading actress and generally help out with routine tasks. Are you interested?"

The unexpected offer stunned me. "Yes ... I guess so." I wondered what "routine tasks" meant, though clearly Principal Boxer saw the opportunity as legitimate.

"One condition, though." I braced for a spoiler. "You can't tell anyone. We're keeping our presence under wraps. Don't want to attract spectators. They slow down production. The local police are going to block off a stretch of beach for us on Saturday. Are you free?"

"Sure. That sounds fine." A rush of excitement filled me. I loved movies. Here was my chance for a first-hand experience.

"Okay. Give me your cell number, and I'll call you tonight with the details."

* * *

When I learned I would be an assistant for Vanessa Jackson, I nearly died. She had been a primary object of my fantasies for a couple of years. I had seen all her films. Now, she lay just beyond the adjoining door, probably having better success at napping than me.

The clock ticked slowly toward dinnertime. Giving up on sleep, I decided to take a shower. In the bathroom mirror I compared my body to Vanessa's. What a mistake. I guess I looked okay, but I couldn't compete with her stunning figure, not to mention her glamor. At school, Alex Conley and some of the other boys pestered me for dates, but I knew what they really wanted. I knew what I wanted, too, and it wasn't them.

Eric had instructed me to dress casually, so I put on a pair of jeans and a green t-shirt and waited for the appointed time, listening all the while for stirrings in the next room. At seven o'clock I went downstairs.

About a dozen men and women had begun to saunter into the private room that had been reserved for the cast and crew. I took a seat at the table. Eric came in and sat next to me. Everyone talked shop and ignored me. I didn't really want to socialize with any of them. But where was Vanessa? Eventually, she breezed in and took her place next to Morgan at the far end of the table. I couldn't hear their words, but she rested her hand on his shoulder, laughing and whispering with him. I passed the meal in silence, trying hard not to stare.

I was too young to legally drink, but the waiter brought wine for everyone. Its sharp fruitiness didn't appeal to me, but after a few sips it went down easier.

Toward the end of the meal, Eric turned to me. "So, how do you like show business?"

"It's okay. I haven't done much, yet."

"Ah … that's the secret. Get paid without doing anything. Hang around the set, pick up the lingo, and make some contacts. Connections will get you further than an acting class."

"I don't want to be an actor."

"Everyone's an actor, sweetie. What's your name, again?"

"Angie."

"Yeah, yeah. Right. I remember now." He pushed his plate away. "I'm going to take a walk on the beach. Want to come?"

Was he hitting on me? I had no interest in him. "I'm kinda tired. Think I'll get some rest … if Vanessa doesn't need me."

"Ah … Vanessa is it? On a first-name basis? Sounds like you two are besties now."

"She asked me to call her—"

"I'm sure. Well, get your rest. See you tomorrow." He seemed to have lost interest pretty quickly.

I returned to my room. The glass of wine, or was it two, had gone to my head. My previous drinking experience had been limited to a couple of beers with Sandy when I slept over at her house. Her folks were broad-minded, unlike my strict, ultra-conservative parents.

I flopped on the bed with the TV remote and began to channel surf. I hit the mute button and lay there, listening through the open window to the ocean's surf, rolling gently upon the sand.

A light tapping woke me. I hadn't meant to fall asleep. Groggily, I rose. The TV, tuned to a shopping channel, silently pitched facial creams—ugh. Only when the tapping ceased did I realize it had been coming from the adjoining door. I staggered over and flung it open, nearly losing my balance. Vanessa stood there in a t-shirt and sweatpants, holding a bottle of wine and two glasses. She looked great.

I blinked and stupidly asked, "Do you need something?"

"Just some company for a little while before bed. May I come in?"

"Of ... of course. I must have dozed off."

She took a seat at one end of a short sofa and sat the wine and glasses on the coffee table. She uncorked the bottle and cast a questioning glance at me. I nodded, and she filled the glasses halfway. My heart pounded. Was this really happening? Could my wildest fantasies be coming true? Did she see through my struggle to remain calm?

She gave me a relaxed smile. "So, how do you like show business?" Those were Eric's exact words at dinner. I was sure he had been hitting on me, but was she?

I took a big sip of wine. "It's fine. I've never met a movie star before."

She laughed. "We're like other people, some good, some bad. Of course, we all have ego issues."

"I'm sure you don't—"

"Oh, don't kid yourself. Everyone lavishes adoration on us. It's really hard not to get full of yourself, though the attention gets tiresome ... sometimes. I'm as guilty as the rest." She shook her head. "What about you? Got a boyfriend?"

"Well, there's Sandy." I hesitated and then blurted out, "She's a girl." Immediately, I regretted it. Damn that wine. What did Vanessa think about our morning on the beach? She must have realized she had aroused my fantasies. Why did I reveal my secret? I had told no one. But it didn't appear to faze her.

"That's lovely. You're so lucky to have figured out your sexuality at such a young age. So many deny their true natures and go through hell until ..." She gazed into her wine glass. "Are you out? Do people know?"

"Not really. I guess some have suspicions. My parents don't know. They'd be in denial even if I told them. Next year, I'll be away at college. I can be myself there."

Vanessa put her hand on the bottle. "Another?"

"Okay." My confession left me feeling exposed. The wine offered an escape from thought.

"You know, Angie, relationships are hard for everyone. I'm trying to make things work with Larry. He's shooting in Europe. I'm sure he has opportunities with women there. I'd like to think he's faithful, but my gut tells me he's not. It's this damn business we're in. It isolates you from the real world." She shook her head. "But I'm sick of talking about me. What's going to happen with you and Sandy after graduation?"

"I don't know. Her parents can afford to send her to an exclusive, private university. I'll have to go to a state college. We want to stay committed to each other, but the distance ..."

"I've been there. My high school romance didn't survive our first semester at the university. You're young. You've got your head together. You'll be fine." She drained her glass. "Well, got to get up early. Thanks for your company." She leaned over and gave me a hug. "Good night."

The soft swoosh of the ocean fed my melancholy. A wave of sadness washed over me, though I couldn't say why. Was it the alcohol? Sleep proved impossible, so I walked down to the beach. The stars and a half moon gave a lunar quality to the landscape. I have often been lonely, but that night the sensation over-powered my senses. I damned the wine again and envisioned Vanessa making love with Larry. What did she see in him?

"Out for a walk?" The words stunned me. I thought I was alone. Between the night and the alcohol, it took a few moments to recognize Eric. What did he want? Why wouldn't he leave me alone? He came closer and put his hand on my shoulder.

"Don't," I said, but he kissed me, and for some unfathomable reason, I let him.

He whispered something I didn't catch, but then repeated, "Let's go to my room."

It felt like an out-of-body experience. I put one foot in front of the other and allowed him to take me back to the hotel. Thank God he was prepared with a condom. The awkward, unsatisfying encounter lacked the tenderness I had known with Sandy. I found refuge in imagining myself as Vanessa and him as Larry. What was so appealing about being with a man? The answer eluded me. It was an episode I vowed to not repeat.

When we finished, I got up and dressed. Eric drifted off to sleep. I doubt he regretted my departure. Back in my room Vanessa's wine bottle still sat on the coffee table. I hoped another glass would help me sleep, but it had the opposite effect.

At breakfast with the cast and crew, Eric ignored me. I sought relief from my hangover with a cup of coffee and likewise avoided eye contact with him. When Vanessa didn't show up, Morgan grumbled about his star's absence.

"Do you want me to check on her?" I offered.

He gave a dismissive wave. "Let her sleep. She can be a bitch if you wake her before she's ready."

I took my coffee down to the beach. The cool Sunday morning breeze blew in off the water. I breathed deeply and replayed my confessional chat with Vanessa. Last night's words sounded stupid in the light of day. What did she think of me? I desired to be near her again but feared I had damaged our relationship.

"Angie?"

I turned to find a blond woman with a cheerful, disarming smile. "Yes."

"Hi, I'm Leslie Watson." She must have seen the confusion in my eyes. "I'm Ms. Jackson's assistant. Thank you so much for filling in for me. I'm sure Ms. Jackson appreciates it, too."

"Am I ... to leave?"

"I'm afraid we no longer require your assistance. I'm much better, now. I'm ready to resume my duties, but thanks again for everything you've done."

"May I say goodbye to Va ... I mean, Ms. Jackson?"

"Let's not disturb her. She's preparing for her scenes today. I'll pass along your farewell. Oh, and I'll have to move into your room, so I can be near when she requires me."

I trudged upstairs and began to pack, pausing periodically to listen at the adjoining door, but I heard nothing.

A deserted lobby greeted me when I went downstairs to turn in my key. I loitered for a few minutes, wishing for someone to say goodbye to. I wanted to feel like I had been part of the company, if only for a short while. It soon dawned on me that everyone had departed for the day's shooting. Feeling discarded, I gave up and went home.

* * *

Sandy and I had a glorious summer, spending lots of days at the beach and many nights of sleepovers at her house. I think her parents knew, and I'm sure mine didn't. In the fall, we went off to separate colleges, vowing to maintain our relationship.

Just before leaving home in August, I received a belated graduation card from Vanessa. Her note wished me luck and expressed hope I would find happiness. She confided that her own love life was in turmoil. That was hardly news. I had seen the gossip in the tabloids. She advised me to avoid a career in show business, though I knew all along that life wasn't for me. I never got paid for that weekend, but some things are more valuable than money, like memories of Vanessa Jackson dancing naked on the beach.

Black Bear Lake

The cops say Danny drowned in Black Bear Lake, but they never found his body. The lake lies secluded in the backwoods of the North Carolina mountains. Its deep, murky waters are shrouded in legend. The locals recite countless tales of supernatural happenings, suicidal lovers, and the like. To get there you had to drive for miles down a narrow dirt track. You couldn't really call it a road. We went there to drink beer and smoke pot.

I remember the last trip with Danny—July 1, 1970. Ted and George came with us, and Danny brought his girlfriend, Ellen. That summer we drove up from our various hometowns and gathered at the small college in western North Carolina we attended. An excursion to Black Bear Lake offered an antidote to the summer doldrums after our sophomore year and a way to blot out the uncertainty of what was to come.

On previous trips, we limited our activity to hiking, but this time Ted prodded us to get out on the water. His father loaned us two canoes, which we strapped to the top of my car. For a couple of hours, we jolted along over uneven terrain and splashed through shallow streams, sometimes barely squeezing through the encroaching undergrowth. On one occasion the thicket hung so low we had to remove the canoes and drag them for a hundred feet or so before securing them once again.

Finally, the lake came into view. Its serene water, surrounded by the graceful blueness of the mountains, never failed to fill me with a sense of peacefulness I have seldom found elsewhere. We unloaded our gear, piled into the canoes, and set out with an abundance of enthusiasm. Paddling, we quickly discovered, is considerably more difficult than it appears in the movies. We were just a bunch of overindulged college kids who had never put in a day of manual labor in our lives, but we goaded each other on and eventually reached our destination, a small island in the middle of the lake.

Danny immediately produced a Frisbee and sent it sailing down the small sandy strip, which served as a miniature beach. Ellen chased it down and flung it back. Ted, George, and I unloaded tents, backpacks, and the all-important cooler. George wasted no time in cracking open a beer. He looked over at me.

"Want one?"

I shook my head. "We've got lots of time. Let's explore first."

Ted gave a nod. "I'll come."

We left George to his beer and struck out. Low, scrubby bushes populated the small island, and a few gnarly trees grew here and there. We quickly reached the opposite shore.

"Not much here," I said.

Ted picked up a stick and swung it aimlessly. "It's just fine."

"Yeah. I guess you're right. Enough room for the five of us, for sure."

By the time we got back, George had joined the Frisbee game. Next to Danny's lean, graceful motions and Ellen's quickness, he looked like a stumbling giant launching his big, awkward body across the sand in an earnest but futile effort to make a catch. When he went sprawling, Ted approached and offered his hand.

"Thanks," George mumbled. "I guess I need another beer."

Ted held up a joint. "Why don't we have a smoke instead?"

The afternoon passed in a blur of pot and beer. George fell asleep, but the rest of us rose dutifully to our feet and began gathering wood for a fire. Danny and Ellen took charge of cooking the burgers while Ted and I stretched out on the sand.

"They say a Cherokee brave drowned his unfaithful lover in the lake ...," Ted began.

"I heard," Ellen interrupted as she flipped the burgers, "that he drowned her because she caught him cheating on her."

"He said, she said," I replied. "There are many versions of that old story. Some say they were newlyweds out for a swim when she caught a cramp, and they both drowned when he tried to save her."

Ted waved off my remark. "Well, an old Indian told me it was the woman that was cheating."

Ellen gave him a skeptical glance. "Yeah, but I'll bet she put the blame on the man."

Danny slapped the face of the guitar he had brought. "I think I'll write a song about it."

"You're too late," I said. "All these old legends have been set to music many times."

"None as good as the tune I'll compose."

"We'll see," I said, with a laugh.

Danny strummed a dissonant chord.

Ted smirked. "Off to a great start."

"Just keeping my mind busy. Tomorrow will—"

"Hush." Ellen's voice was a whisper. "Let's not

think about tomorrow."

It was too late. Danny's remark had shattered the mood. An uneasy quiet fell upon us, broken only by the sizzling of the burgers. Though we tried to avoid it, the randomness that would determine our futures weighed heavily on our minds. Finally, Ellen took up the last of the burgers.

"Shall we wake George for dinner?" I asked.

Ted grinned mischievously. "Let him sleep."

Ellen smiled. "You're bad boys." She bent over George and gave him a kiss on his forehead. He awoke startled and looked around in wide-eyed bewilderment.

"You just died and went to heaven," Ted joked. Everyone laughed.

Afterwards, Danny picked up his guitar and played, while we listened drowsily. Ellen sung softly to some of the popular songs. The fire popped and crackled in accompaniment. How could life be any better?

Darkness comes quickly when there's no electricity. The dying fire and our single lantern provided enough light to set up the tents and roll out our sleeping bags.

Danny surveyed the moonless night. "How about a swim before bedtime?" Without waiting for a response, he stripped off his clothes and plunged naked into the cold, dark water. I didn't feel the urge to jump in. Even in the summer those mountain lakes were frigid, especially after sundown, but a moment later Ellen rose, slipped out of her clothes, and followed him.

"All right!" exclaimed George, rising to his feet in lusty excitement.

"Hold on, George." Ted reached up and grabbed his elbow. "Let them have some fun."

George looked down at Ted and me. I nodded my agreement. "Aww ...," he complained and dropped onto the sand with a grunt.

Ten minutes later, Danny's lanky form and Ellen's petite body emerged, shivering in the cool night air. They wrapped themselves in a couple of towels and sat close to the fire. We passed around another joint. After the last toke, Danny and Ellen retreated to their tent. The rest of us turned in, too. The ground was hard, but we were tired and sleep came easily despite the nightly insect chorus.

We drove back to campus the following morning to face what we all dreaded. For any trip, returning is less fun than going. In the summer of 1970, it proved to be especially true. The journey passed largely in silence—five teens crammed tightly together in a small space, each alone with his or her own thoughts.

On campus, we bought a newspaper at the news-stand next to the post office and anxiously scanned the draft lottery numbers. I breathed a sigh of relief when I read 272 by my birthdate, plenty high enough to avoid induction. Ted, after checking his number, looked up and gave a grin, the tension dropping from his face.

George frowned. "It's 110," he murmured. "What do you think?"

I paused before answering. "Could go either way. What's your birthday, Danny?"

He glanced over my shoulder. "Shit. May twenty-ninth."

A heavy silence descended over our little band. Ellen began to cry. Danny put his arm around her.

Together they walked away as if they were one instead of two.

George glanced at his watch. "I gotta go and meet Walt," he said and hurried off.

Ted and I shuffled over to the student union and plopped down on a bench out front. Ted spoke first.

"He'll get a student deferment."

"Maybe. His grades aren't so hot. If he flunks out ..."

"Yeah, I know what you mean. This should motivate him to work harder, but I could see it having the opposite effect on Danny."

"You might be right, Ted. After all, a deferment would only delay the inevitable."

"Yeah, I guess. Deferments run out eventually, don't they? I feel guilty. We were lucky and Danny wasn't. How do you feel?"

"Me? Suddenly, I feel old."

* * *

We drifted back to our separate summer lives. Danny didn't return for fall semester, though his induction wasn't scheduled until February. He sent a letter saying he intended to enlist. "The sooner I go in, the sooner I'll get out," he wrote. Ellen returned to school, but we didn't see her much. Ted and I roomed together that semester in an off-campus apartment. On a cool, crisp morning in late October a knock on my door awakened me. I thought Ted had forgotten his key again, but in the doorway stood a deputy sheriff.

He confirmed my identity and asked, "Do you know a Daniel Forsyth?"

"Yes," I responded, with trepidation. At first, I feared Danny had been caught with a bag of pot. The sweat began to bead on my forehead and collect under my armpits. I tried not to think about the stash in my dresser.

"I have some bad news. Your friend is missing. We found his car up at Black Bear Lake."

"He may be hiking in the area." I felt relief that I wasn't the object of his visit. "He's probably with friends up there. I'm surprised he didn't call me. He usually does when he's coming up."

"The thing is," the officer continued, "we found the canoe he rented. Was he a good swimmer?"

A knot of dread formed in the pit of my stomach. I tried to deny it. "Yeah, real good. You think he drowned?"

"It's looking that way. He should have returned the canoe two days ago and his girlfriend hasn't heard from him."

Numbness washed over my body. "He wouldn't drown," I stated with certainty, for the officer's benefit and my own.

"Do you know if he was depressed?" The officer's voice was flat and routine.

"Suicide? Not Danny." My words sounded too loud. "He's not the type."

"His girlfriend, uh ..." the deputy checked his notepad, "Ellen Barker, says he's been moody."

"Well, yeah. He's got his worries as we all do." I decided to not mention his draft status, perhaps due to a generational distrust of authority. Besides, the deputy appeared intent on telling me things that couldn't be true. Why should I give him any information? Anyway, I didn't see how it would help find

Danny.

"When did you see him last?"

"July."

After a couple more questions, the officer concluded the interview. He jotted down a few notes and started to leave, but turned back.

"Give us a call if you hear from him, okay?" He handed his card to me.

For several minutes, I stood there, too stunned to move. I stared at his card and tried to come to terms with what he had said. It seemed unreal. My phone rang, stirring me from my thoughts. I guessed before answering that Ted or George was calling to tell me what I already knew.

The weeks passed without news. Slowly we began to acknowledge our worst fears. George, Ted, and I mulled over a variety of speculations. Did he drown by accident or by intent? In a burst of unsupported optimism, we concocted the idea that he faked it and went into hiding or possibly fled to Canada. We had no evidence for any of our theories. In time, we came to accept the official narrative of a "probable drowning," though we often wondered if the local authorities lacked the incentive to fully investigate the disappearance of a long-haired college kid.

We did our best to console Ellen, but before Thanksgiving she withdrew from school and returned home. George quit at the end of the semester and enlisted. To "take Danny's place," he said. I tried to talk him out of it, but George had a stubborn streak once he made up his mind. He never came back from Vietnam.

* * *

The following summer, Ted and I made the trek to Black Bear Lake. In vain, we sought to relive the pleasures of summers past, but joy eluded us. We missed the camaraderie of our friends. Without the joking and singing that sustained us the previous summer, paddling to the island took an eternity. We quickly tired of chasing the Frisbee, which seemed to consciously drift just beyond our reach. The ritual of making a fire and cooking burgers became a quotidian task. Afterwards, we settled down with a joint and a couple of beers to watch the sunset. Ted broke the silence.

"It's only been a year, but it seems like a lifetime."

"Yeah, I feel so much older."

Ted inhaled a long toke. "Danny's out there somewhere."

I nodded. "I suppose he'll become one more chapter in the legend of Black Bear Lake."

"Yeah, I think he'd like that." Ted's grin was barely visible in the fading light. "Don't you?"

I felt Ted was wrong. Being a live person is better than a being a dead legend, but I didn't contradict his romantic notion. We talked a while longer, our conversation meandering through a cannabis haze. Eventually sleep came, interrupted only by the need to urinate.

* * *

Ted and I pursued our studies, and both graduated a semester late. They say you can do college in four years, but a lot of my friends took longer. Some never finished. After graduation Ted got a bank job in Charlotte, and I went to work for a university in Raleigh. Only a few hours of interstate highway separated us, but as time passed, we saw each other less. Neither of us fully embraced the social media revolution that has helped succeeding generations stay in touch with virtually everyone they ever knew. However, we managed to attend each other's wedding. Then came parenthood, kids, and their soccer games and gymnastics. I knew we were micromanaging our kids' lives, but you fall into the pattern of your times.

It's astounding how having children makes the decades fly. Memories dim with the passing years. Faces are remembered, but names forgotten. Details get fuzzy, and the chronology of life becomes scrambled. Often, I fail to recall who was with me at certain times, but that day at Black Bear Lake in the summer of 1970 remained crystal clear.

My retirement, which had seemed so distant for so long, suddenly loomed close. Freedom from my working life finally lay before me with its fickle promises of copious spare time. I planned to spend my days leisurely reading all the books I had never found the time for, doing a little writing myself, and taking a couple of special vacations with my wife.

* * *

One day out of the blue, Ted called. It had been more than a year since we last spoke. We had grown apart in tastes and politics. Our common ground remained rooted in the past.

"What's up?" I asked.

"You remember Ellen, Danny's girl?"

"Sure."

"I just heard from Walt. You remember him, right?

He says Ellen is living in the backwoods of Canada—way out west, north of Vancouver. She's got a cabin in the middle of nowhere, and she's hooked up with some musician."

"Good for her. She always had a thing for musicians. I worried about her after Danny died."

"Let's go see her." Ted's tone took on an enthusiastic edge.

"Whoa. I can't drop everything and fly to Vancouver. We haven't seen Ellen in … forty years. I wouldn't have anything to say to her."

"What if he turned out to be Danny?"

"Who? Who do you mean?"

"That musician she's shacked up with … could be Danny."

"You're crazy, Ted."

"They never found his body."

"But we would have heard from him. When President Carter granted that universal amnesty in the mid-seventies, he would have come home."

"Maybe not, if Ellen was with him, or if he felt guilty about George. You know, enlisting in his place."

"You're crazy," I repeated. "You're getting old and feeble-minded like me."

"Maybe that's so, but I want to go back in time and make everything come out right."

"Sure, Ted, we all feel that way. Hey, next summer after I retire, let's take a trip to Black Bear Lake, for old times' sake."

"Okay, old man. I'll see you then."

* * *

I picked up Ted in Charlotte the following summer

and drove to our old stomping grounds. The trip began with small talk but soon turned to the "good ole days" and then to Danny.

"Maybe he skipped off to Canada." Ted's words smacked of self-delusion rather than conviction.

"Yeah, maybe, but Black Bear Lake is deep and muddy. He might be there."

"They didn't find him. He could have faked his suicide."

"You sound like a conspiracy nut. He wouldn't have done that," I countered. "I don't think the cops did a great job of investigating his death. He meant nothing to them. But even if they made the effort, they may not have found him. In those days they didn't have the technology they do today."

"But we know Ellen is in Canada. Walt made it sound like she's living off the grid. Why would she be there if not to be with Danny?"

"I don't know, Ted. Who can say why some folks end up in the places they do?"

Ted shook his head. "If I was Danny, I'd feel guilty about George. I don't know if I could face everyone."

"Guilt's a funny thing. Sometimes I feel like it's my fault for failing to talk George out of joining up even though I tried. But it's crazy to think about changing the past. You have to live with it."

In a small town near campus, we rented a canoe, strapped it to the roof of my car, and headed for the lake. To our surprise, a newly graveled road took the adventure out of the journey. At the lake shore a parking lot and canoe rental stand greeted us. A party of Boy Scouts occupied several picnic tables. On the surface of the water, a dozen or so paddlers worked their crafts back and forth.

"Damn," I said. "I guess we didn't need to haul a canoe up here."

We stood for a few moments, not knowing what to do next.

"It's changed a lot." Ted didn't try to hide his disappointment. "It's too goddamn wholesome. They've practically ruined it. The worst thing is that damned road. Getting here used to be half the fun."

We strolled around the site and discovered a dozen cabins had been constructed beyond the picnic tables. Meanwhile, the scouts had broken into teams and the scoutmasters were laying down rules for some sort of game.

"That's really roughing it." I nodded toward the cabins. "They probably have electricity and running water."

"Next thing you know they'll put in an RV parking lot," Ted grunted.

We leaned against my car and surveyed the scene. I couldn't deny everyone there was having fun, except us—two grumpy old farts disenchanted with the unexpected changes to the paradise they had hoped to reclaim.

Ted broke the spell. "Is Danny out there, or in Canada? What do you really think?"

"I don't know, but either way, he didn't want to be found."

"I suppose you're right," Ted conceded with a sigh.

After a few minutes of indecision, we got back in my car and drove away. Memories of times past and songs sung long ago surged up within us. We laughed at our youthful follies and sang the old songs all the way home.

One Night in Las Vegas

Jackson and I pushed our way through the crowded casino to the table where Marcos dealt blackjack. We stood among the spectators, watching as his deck diminished. When a dozen or so cards remained, he scooped up the discards and began to shuffle.

Jackson edged forward and gave the sign. Marcos's sharp eyes caught the movement. Jackson held up two fingers and tilted his head toward me. Marcos nodded in response and from his vest pocket drew two green tokens. Jackson stepped closer and accepted the tokens. Marcos gestured toward the bar and mouthed "Frankie." Jackson backed away, pulling me with him.

"See, I told you." He handed me one of the tokens. "You can get anything in Vegas."

I examined my token. It resembled a typical gambling chip except for a large "2" on both sides. Jackson pocketed his. I did the same with mine.

Saturday night brought in an amazing variety of patrons. Tourists overwhelmingly dominated the floor, but boozers and cruisers mingled as well, along with serious gamblers. A redheaded woman, wearing a tight, electric blue dress, screamed as we passed the craps table. Was it a cry of pleasure or despair? I couldn't tell. We made our way to the bar, and Jackson motioned to the tall, slender bartender.

"Frankie working?"

The bartender shifted his gaze toward the other end of the bar where a muscular man with a handlebar moustache served margaritas to a pair of giggling young women. After a few moments he escaped their exuberance, and the tall bartender whispered to him. Frankie gave us a long stare before approaching.

Jackson slid his token onto the counter. I followed suit. Frankie examined the tokens before depositing them in a small jar by the cash register where four others already resided.

Jackson gave me a nudge. "Looks like we'll have company for dinner."

Frankie leaned over the counter and in a low voice said simply, "Midnight."

I checked my watch. "We've got a couple of hours to kill. What do you want to do?"

"Don't drink," Jackson advised. "It'll spoil everything, and we can't afford to gamble away our fee." He patted the breast pocket of his jacket and surveyed the room with a scowl. "These tourists come seeking some sort of unique adventure." He made no effort to hide the disdain in his voice. "But they all have the same experience, really. They drink too much, lose a little money, and go home. They tell their friends and relatives how much fun they had. The kicker is most will come back and do it again."

"We're different." I looked to Jackson for validation. "Our experience will be unique."

He frowned and glanced away. "A rare experience perhaps, though not unique. There are no more unique experiences. Rare is the best you can hope for."

I felt let down. Jackson's sudden, matter-of-fact pessimism took some of the luster off our quest. After all, it was he who first proposed the idea. He talked it up and made a big deal over the lengths we had to go to. His contagious energy swept me up at the outset. Now with the end in sight, his mood seemed to be souring. Had the journey become more important than the goal? Considering the time and money invested, his lackluster attitude in the final hours puzzled me.

I wandered off and spent my time observing casino patrons at slot machines mechanically pressing the spin button, boredom etched on their faces. Almost no one bothered to use the lever, though it still adorned most of the machines. Shortly before twelve, I strolled back to the bar. Jackson waited there with Frankie and a well-dressed, elderly couple.

At the stroke of midnight, we were joined by a middle-aged man and an attractive woman in her early twenties. The young woman with her big hair, short skirt, and low-cut blouse jingled with bling as she walked. Her short, stocky companion, dressed in a rumpled suit, chomped absentmindedly on an unlit cigar. The pair were a Vegas cliché, right out of the movies.

The seven of us trooped through the lobby and down a hallway next to the restrooms. Frankie left us in a room not much bigger than an elevator. In the uncomfortable closeness I stared at the floor. When I raised my head to speak, Jackson shook his head. A long fifteen minutes later Frankie reappeared. The elderly man handed an envelope to him. Jackson and the other man did the same. Frankie slipped them, unopened, into his pocket.

We passed through a series of utility corridors until we stood before a royal-blue door. Frankie produced a key and let us in. A table and six chairs occupied the center of the otherwise bare room. Each place was set with a plate, silverware, napkins, and a glass of water.

As soon as we took our seats, the door at the far end opened, and a waiter entered, balancing six covered dishes on a large tray. He placed them before us and withdrew. A few anxious moments passed before Jackson removed his cover.

The shell-less, roasted turtle steamed with aromatic spices and swam in a pale brown sauce. The creature had two heads. The sight, though expected, unnerved me. After taking a deep breath, I summoned the strength to uncover my dish. Mine also had two heads, but surprisingly, it had three front legs. The others revealed their plates, but I couldn't bring myself to look.

Next to me, Jackson calmly sliced off a piece, took a tentative bite, and then proceeded to consume his entire portion in short order. The man with the cigar, sitting across from me, took a small bite and began to gag. He coughed into his napkin, pushed back his chair, and hurried from the room. His girlfriend gave a shrug and resumed dining. The elderly couple ate slowly, savoring every bite.

I cut a piece and forced myself to swallow it. With the significant cost weighing on my mind, I had another, chasing it with a big gulp of water. Closing my eyes, I gave up and struggled to banish the image from my mind while anxiously waiting for the others to conclude their meals. It took the elderly couple twenty minutes. Finally, they laid down their utensils. We sat without speaking until Frankie reappeared and led us back to the casino floor.

The elderly couple immediately sought out the craps table. When the young woman's companion didn't show, Jackson moved in and struck up a conversation. I hoped he knew what he was doing. She looked like a hooker to me, but in Vegas it's difficult to be certain.

I headed straight for the bar, ordered a double whiskey, and downed it. For a few minutes I simmered with anger, first at Jackson and then at myself, for being caught up in his crazy, frivolous quest. After a second round, my resentment eased. We came for an unusual experience, and we found it, though the extravagant cost rankled me.

I had started on my third whiskey when Jackson appeared and clapped me on the shoulder. He slapped a slip of paper down on the bar in front of me and winked. I saw a phone number etched in purple ink before he picked it up and slipped it into his pocket. Sliding onto the stool beside me, he ordered a drink. He remained silent until it arrived and had taken his first sip.

"Siamese twin turtle ... or conjoined, I suppose, is the politically correct term. How many people can boast of a dinner like that? Very few I'll wager, but you can't tell anyone. The animal rights groups will raise hell if they get wind of it. That'll end it for everyone."

"I-I'm s-sure you're r-right," I stammered.

Our mission fulfilled, Jackson's enthusiasm resurfaced. He expounded on the subtle taste, tender texture, and superb seasoning, though clearly what he really relished was the taboo nature of the adventure. I found the whole affair unsettling, yet I can't say the turtle tasted bad, kind of like chicken, I guess.

Inheriting Dad

Death has always fascinated me. During my child-hood, it only happened to old people, usually distant relatives. Later, it came at me in the news when the famous died. In my senior year of high school, a car crash took the lives of two classmates. While at college, a student in my accounting class drowned. Two years ago, my mother passed away. Now, my father was dead.

I dropped my cigarette in the steamy summer heat of the parking lot and crushed it out. Remembering my father's dislike of littering, never mind the habit of smoking itself, I picked it up. He still held sway over my actions even now. It would be easy enough to dispose of the butt inside.

Winston's Funeral Home, a low, squat building I knew well, loomed ominously, a visceral reminder of the fate that awaits us all. Surrounded by a decade of urban resurgence, it retained an aura of malignant indifference to the human condition.

In the past, I generally entered by the side door, which opened to the parking lot, but today I walked around to the front. In the serene coolness of the foyer, a slow-moving elderly man greeted me. He looked ready for the grave himself.

"Harris," I replied, in response to his unspoken question. When he reached out to shake my hand, I quickly shifted the cigarette butt to my left palm. Afterwards, I feared it had left its stale odor on his hand.

He guided me to a room filled with an abundance of thickly scented flowers. The familiar fragrances brought back childhood memories of solemn adults speaking in somber tones of the recently departed. A sudden, irrational feeling came over me as if my father's spirit lurked among the floral arrangements, waiting to emerge and tell me how to live my life. I pushed those thoughts aside, but where was he? Had I arrived too early? I took a seat on a sofa and waited.

I guess my relationship with him resembled that of many other fathers and their sons. It must have been hard for him, too. My failed marriage and less than stellar business career bitterly disappointed him. When I turned thirty last year, his vocal criticisms lessened, but his disapproval of my life remained an unspoken barrier between us. Still, he truly meant well and wanted the best for me. I would probably have been as hard on my son if my marriage had not ended before we had children. Thank God for that.

For all his faults as a father, he had none of the social vices like drinking or swearing, though he looked down on others who yielded to those failings. Conservative in his politics, he complained bitterly of government handouts and backed up his convictions with a strong work ethic. He loved the outdoors but remained suspicious of the environmental movement.

Now it had all changed. His absence felt both liberating and frustrating. He was frozen in time, never again to be argued with, persuaded, or otherwise brought to any compromise in our long and tumultuous relationship. No, it wasn't over, but it had changed in ways with which I doubted I would ever come to terms. On the other hand, I had begun to feel a tingling of emotional freedom that had not been possible before. I didn't quite know how to embrace it.

A fly buzzed among the nearby flowers, the only movement in the otherwise still room. I recalled my father's extreme dislike of flies and other insects. His appreciation of nature did not extend to tiny bugs that bit and stung.

A few moments later, the fly circled my head, reminding me why we call them pests. I waved the bothersome insect away. In my mind, I saw my father's familiar gesture performing the identical action, and with it I heard his mutterings of annoyance as if he were whispering in my ear. Closing my eyes, I tried to clear my thoughts. A wave of dizziness washed over me, and I tried to stand. The room tilted, and I felt myself sliding from the sofa. I don't remember hitting the floor.

Gradually, I became aware of the low murmur of voices. I slowly opened my eyes and found myself lying on the sofa. Six or seven men huddled in the center of the room, none of them looking at me.

I eased myself to a sitting position. The movement caused heads to turn. A tall, gray-haired man hurried to my side. He put his hand on my shoulder.

"How are you feeling?" His smooth, velvety voice floated languidly in the space between us.

"I'm sorry. I must have fainted. It's been difficult."

"Uh ... yes, I'm sure." He cleared his throat and continued. "We here at Winston's would like you to know we're terribly sorry about all this and will be glad to do anything we can for you."

I couldn't think of anything I wanted him to do. I

only desired to get some rest, make it through the funeral on Saturday, and return to my routine.

"In sixty-four years of service nothing like this has ever happened." The man exuded a somber, apologetic tone. "I'm sure you will understand. If you could—"

"Wait a minute, what are you talking about? I passed out. That must happen all the time in your line of business."

He looked uneasy. My own thoughts so preoccupied me I hadn't noticed, but something was wrong. He glanced down and said something I didn't catch. Scanning the room, I saw the others had withdrawn. My heart felt heavy with the dread of impending bad news.

"I, uh ... I'm sorry to have to, uh ... tell you this," he stuttered, "but your father is alive."

Sinking back on the couch, I tried to comprehend his words. A heart attack had killed my father yesterday, mercifully ending a long period of declining health. The man continued to speak, but I only heard snatches of what he said.

"... hospital failed to ... naturally we couldn't have known ... for the best, I guess, under the circumstances ..."

"Wait, I don't understand," I mumbled, rising to my feet. "Where is he? What happened to him?"

"Please be seated, Mr. Harris," the gray-haired man purred. "Mr. Winston has been informed. He'll be here soon."

"Who are you?" I managed to ask. "And what have you done with my father?"

"Mr. Harris, uh, well, uh there's been a dreadful mistake. Your father's not dead. He's still at the hospital. The doctors made an error. They're only human, you know."

"He can't be alive." I shook my head. "The hospital called and ..."

The gray-haired man looked toward the door and cleared his throat. He started to speak, but closed his mouth and made a vague gesture.

"My father is uh ... not actually dead." My words sounded small. "Is that what you're telling me?"

"I guess so. I mean yes, he is alive. As I said, the hospital made some mistakes. I'm sorry. I know this must be a shock. I hope he'll recover."

"You mean he's going to get well?"

"Uh ... no. I mean, that's for the doctors to say. Would you like to go to the hospital?"

"I don't know. I guess so."

"We can have someone drive you, if you like." That seemed like a good idea.

The trip to the hospital passed in silence. The driver serenely steered the long, funereal limo through the streets. We passed Trinity Towers, an upscale apartment complex. When I was a kid, Trinity Park existed there. On hot summer days I waded in its shallow creek, which wound lazily among the shady oaks and sweetgums.

Turning my thoughts from the past to the present, I mulled over the hospital's mistake in declaring my father deceased. And what bureaucratic snafu kept them from informing me right away once they discovered their blunder?

It seemed incredible, but I recalled news items last year when, at a hospital in California, a minor operation resulted in a comatose patient, and a doctor in Michigan had amputated the wrong arm of a wounded soldier. I shuddered at the thought.

At the hospital, someone guided me through the maze of corridors until I stood before the bed where my father lay. Tubes and wires connected him to an array of impressive machines, which hummed steadily and emitted occasional beeps.

He looked dead. I detected no rise and fall of breath. His body had sunk down into the mattress, making him look rather flat. Nurses and technicians bustled by, taking no notice of me. Later, a nurse took me to an office where I sat in a chair and waited. Eventually, a doctor arrived. He wore a standard white lab coat on his large frame and entered stroking his bushy moustache.

"Hi, Mr. Harris, I'm Dr. Hadley." He took a deep breath. "I am afraid I have bad news. Your father is a very sick man." A litany of ailments followed, each worse than the previous. "Frankly, I'm amazed he's still alive. There's nothing you can do here. Go home. Take it easy for a few days. Stay home from work if you can."

"But Doctor, what happened? How could you have thought he was dead?"

Dr. Hadley hesitated and then launched into an overly detailed recitation of hospital procedures, emphasizing various safeguards. "So, you see the system worked," he concluded. "The only mistake was a clerical one. Our staff, in an effort to keep you up to date, notified you before we had complete information."

His explanation did not answer my question, but I sensed it was the best I could expect. I decided to take his advice and get some rest. The driver from the funeral home reappeared. He escorted me to the car and drove me to my apartment. Once there, I fell into bed fully dressed and slept soundly.

My cell phone woke me. I blinked against the morning sun, streaming through my bedroom window.

"Hello," I croaked.

"Charlie?" It was my ex-wife.

"Yeah Liz, it's me." I coughed and cleared my throat.

"Charlie, I heard about your dad. I'm awfully sorry. Is there anything I can do? Are you okay?"

"Yeah, I'm okay I guess." I paused. "He's not dead, you know." Silence lingered at the other end of the line. I wished for a cigarette.

"Charlie, of course he'll always be a part of you, but you need—"

"Dammit Liz, I mean he's not dead, and don't tell me what I need."

"I don't understand. Why are you acting like this?"

"How am I supposed to act? First, I'm told my father is dead, and then I'm told he's alive. It's like a nightmare."

"You mean he's really alive?" Her voice took on a cheery tone. "I was told he had … uh, passed away. Then it's all good news," she chirped.

"I don't know, Liz. I mean he'll just die again, I suppose."

"Again, Charlie? Are you okay? I can come by tonight after the exhibition."

"Oh, that's right, your show's tonight, isn't it? It's okay. I'll probably go to bed early, and tomorrow I'll go into the office and catch up on a few things. Don't bother coming by."

"Oh Charlie, you're smart enough to get a better

job. I mean—"

"Goddamnit, Liz! Please let me decide about my job. You're—"

"Charlie, I'm only trying to help you."

"Don't try to help. Let me handle things."

"Well, okay. Call me if you need."

"Right. If I need …" I switched off my phone before she could respond.

She meant well, but our conversations always left me feeling inadequate. I had a cigarette and a shower and then another cigarette. My cell phone buzzed again.

"Mr. Harris?"

"Yeah."

"This is Dr. Hadley at the hospital. I'm calling to see how you're doing and to update you on your father's condition."

"How is he?"

"Not too well, I'm afraid. He's still in intensive care. I want to express apologies from all of us at the hospital for the confusion yesterday. Can you come by this morning on your way to work? There are some forms to be signed."

"Yeah. But first I've got to pick up my car at the funeral home."

"Uh … right, Mr. Harris. I see. Ask for me when you arrive, okay?"

"Sure. I'll be there soon."

I had a bagel and a much-needed cup of coffee. While I waited for the taxi, I thought about checking my email but had another cigarette instead.

By the time I retrieved my car and reached the hospital, I had begun to dread the beginning of a new "death watch." It had been hard the first time. Now, it seemed to be a monumental, but unavoidable, chore. I hoped it would be mercifully quick.

This time Dr. Hadley did not keep me waiting. He sat at his desk backed by a wall of framed degrees and awards. Shuffling through a stack of papers, he offered a grim prognosis although Dad was breathing a little easier. Just when I thought the session had concluded, he opened a folder containing several forms.

"Mr. Harris, I would appreciate it if you could take a few moments to read these and sign in the places I've marked." He glanced away as he slid them over to me.

"What are these?"

"They are standard waivers. It's to clarify the situation." His calm, measured tone did not hide his uneasiness.

It took me a moment to realize he feared I might sue the hospital. That had not occurred to me. After all, it wasn't like they caused my father's death. "These aren't necessary."

"In these cases, it's usually best to get things down in writing."

"These cases? Does this happen often?" I found myself amused by his worries and by my apparently superior legal position. No wonder he didn't make me wait this time.

"I'll take them home and read over them," I said with some enjoyment.

"I recommend that we take care of this now. It's for the best. You'll want to put all this behind you, so you can devote your full attention to your father's needs."

"I'll take them home. I would like to see my father now."

Dr. Hadley frowned, but walked with me to the elevator and pressed the up arrow.

"Be sure to get those forms signed tonight. It's always best to get the paperwork out of the way, so we all can focus on the important task of helping your father."

I shook his cool, dry hand and got on the elevator. On the seventh floor, I walked down to the intensive care unit. Dad was, as I expected, unconscious. He looked the same as yesterday. I still failed to detect any signs of life. However, the equipment sustaining him hummed with vitality. I took the rhythmic beeps to be a sign of stability. Fluids flowed through tubes like blood through veins. I stood there for a few minutes listening to the machinery of his life and watching the various screens display their incomprehensible graphs. I was of no use, so I left and went to work.

At the office, my co-workers offered condolences for my father's death. I nodded in response, lacking the energy to explain. Thompson stopped by just as I had begun to scan through my email.

"Hang in there, old man." He slapped me on the back. "We're okay here if you need more time off."

"Thanks, but I don't think Sawyer will see it that way. He doesn't believe in time off."

"For Christ's sake, when a man's father dies, you've got to allow him a little slack."

"He's not dead," I sighed.

"What do you mean? We all heard ..."

"It was a mistake."

"That's great, Charlie." Thompson turned his attention to the file folder in his hands.

I shrugged. "Maybe, but I don't think he'll get any

better."

"You never know. The doctors can do some pretty amazing things these days."

"You're right about that." He failed to notice my cynical tone.

"Go home, Charlie." He finally returned his gaze to me. "You're not ready to come back."

"Perhaps you're right. Tell Sawyer I'll check my email from home. He can call me if anything important comes up."

I got home around noon, had a sandwich for lunch, and watched the local news on TV. Why wasn't my father in the news? The hospital probably managed to hush things up. Just as well, the media was the last thing I needed in my life. I lost the evening to a few bourbons, a half a pack of cigarettes, and a couple of old movies on a cable network.

The following morning, I called in sick and then phoned my sister.

"Hey, Anne."

"Hello, Charlie."

"Look, I should have called sooner, but things have been a little crazy."

"Yeah, I'm sure they have."

"More than a little crazy, I guess. Dad's not actually dead."

"Really? What do you mean? Did the hospital make a mistake?"

"Yeah." I wondered how she could take it so casually.

"So, he's still alive? Well, that's good. The funeral was going to be difficult for us. Bill is so busy and the kids …"

"Doesn't it sound strange to you?"

"Well, the doctors are only human."

"Do you think you might come by the hospital to see him?"

"I don't know, Charlie. Those places always depress me. Is he awake?"

"No."

"Do they think he'll wake up?"

"I guess not."

"Then what good would it do?"

"It would help me."

"How, Charlie? You needn't be there either. They'll call if he wakes up."

"Someone should be there."

"The kids take so much energy, and Bill is working overtime this month. I can't do it. Listen, you call me if there's any change. I've got to run now."

After hanging up, I felt a rising anger at Anne's lack of interest. I wished Dad's illness would bring us together, but the gulf between us remained. We never had a falling-out, but as grownups we didn't have anything in common despite growing up in the same household.

I dutifully drove to the hospital and found my father's condition unchanged, though fewer tubes were attached. Was it a good sign or a bad one? I didn't know. Once again, I could do nothing for him. I guess Anne had a point. As I made my way toward the elevator, Dr. Hadley hailed me and asked about the forms. I promised to return them soon without meaning it.

My phone buzzed as I was having lunch at my apartment. I hesitated, but answered it with some reluctance.

"Mr. Harris?"

"Yes."

"This is Roy Wilcox with Hoffman Mutual Insurance. I need to verify some information about your late father."

I groaned. When the hospital had called to inform me of Dad's death, I promptly notified his lawyer and the insurance company, desiring to speed through the legal process. I suspected halting the bureaucratic juggernaut would prove to be a more difficult task.

"He's not dead."

There was a pause. "Mr. Harris, you notified us of his ... uh, passing."

"It's a mistake."

"Really?" Skepticism colored his question.

"It was a mistake. He's not dead. Just forget about it."

"I'm afraid we'll need a written statement. We have a form—"

"Send the goddamn form!"

"Please, Mr. Harris, there's no need for that kind of language."

"Go to hell!" I shouted and terminated the call. I would have to contact him eventually to sort it out, but it felt good to be angry.

I went downstairs to check my mailbox. Among the regular bills and ads, a letter from Winston's Funeral Home turned up. I opened it and found a bill for "services." It was so absurd that I laughed until tears streamed down my face. I tossed it into the folder with Dr. Hadley's forms.

The following morning, I called the office and said I would work from home for the rest of the week. I got the sense my value to the company had become suspect. After breakfast I made my daily trip to the hospital. When Dr. Hadley flagged me down, I began to devise excuses for not signing the forms, but he had other things on his mind.

"Mr. Harris, there has been improvement in your father's condition."

A few minutes later, we stood by Dad's bed. He looked the same to me. Dr. Hadley pointed to the monitors and spoke in medical jargon designed to make me feel inferior. It all meant nothing until I saw Dad's hand twitch. I was stunned. The process of his dying seemed as if it would stretch on forever. We went to Dr. Hadley's office to talk.

"His condition is more stable now, but don't get your hopes up. He's still quite ill."

"Doctor, he's gone from being dead to being 'quite ill.' I'd say that is a big improvement."

"Well ... yes, but we're not sure he'll progress from this point."

"God, he would have hated this drawn out affair."

"I'm sure you're right, but we're committed to helping him as long as we can."

"Do you seriously think that dragging this out is helping him?"

"We must do everything we can."

"And then some," I muttered under my breath.

"Excuse me?"

"Nothing. Just do your best. I'm sure he will take a turn for the worse soon."

"I'm afraid that's the most likely scenario."

I quickly concluded the discussion, but not before Dr. Hadley reminded me about the importance of signing the waiver forms. I lied to him again.

After dinner that evening, Liz phoned.

"Charlie, I'm sorry about the other day. You know

I just want you to be happy."

"Forget it. Don't worry about me."

"But I am worried. I …"

"Liz, please let me live my own life."

"Sorry. How's your dad?"

"It appears he's getting better."

"That's great. Do you think they will let him come home?"

"I don't know. I don't think so. He's too sick."

"If I can do anything, give me a call."

"I doubt anyone can help him."

"I mean for you too, Charlie."

"I guess not, Liz. Thanks, though. I'm sure it's only a matter of time."

"Okay, Charlie, but if things change and you need me, don't hesitate to call."

"Thanks, I will."

After a few minutes, I tried my sister's number, but she didn't answer. I wasn't sure what I wanted to say to her anyway.

In the morning, I opened my laptop and discovered it was Friday. Where had the week gone? I logged in to my email, caught up with some correspondence, and reworked a couple of spreadsheets. When I finished, I felt a little better about my job responsibilities. Then Dr. Hadley called.

"Good news, Mr. Harris. Your father is awake."

"What? Really? That's not possible, is it?"

"It's a miracle. His condition is much better today. Of course, it may not last."

"What does this mean?"

"He's interacting with the nurses, though he hasn't spoken yet. His color is returning. If this keeps up, he may be moved to a regular room."

"I can't believe it. Are you sure?"

"Of course." A few days ago, they were sure he was dead.

"I'll be in shortly."

But I didn't go. Somehow, it was harder now. If I waited, perhaps I would soon get a call saying he had relapsed. I stayed home and tried to take a nap, but sleep eluded me. Around dinner time, I called the hospital. At first, there seemed to be confusion at the nurse's station. I was sure Dad must have died. Eventually, a nurse came on the line and told me he had been moved to a regular room.

That evening, I called my sister again.

"Anne, Dad's out of intensive care. He might actually get well enough to leave the hospital."

"That's nice, Charlie. I'll try to come and see him when he gets home."

"I'm not sure he'll come home. He'll have to have assistance."

"A nursing home? That's expensive."

"Maybe he could stay with one of us."

"Gosh, we're too crowded. I mean the laundry is about to push me out the front door, and the kids with all their friends ... It's too loud and crazy here. What about your place? It's just you, and you've got that extra bedroom, right?"

"Well, yes, but I'm at work all day. For him, it would be like living alone."

"Isn't there someone who can check on him during the day, a neighbor or someone?"

"God, I don't even know my neighbors."

"Look, I've got to go. Bill will be home anytime. Keep me in touch with what's happening with Dad."

After I hung up, I searched my memory for occasions when my sister and I were close. None came to mind. When she reached high school, various clubs and sleepovers at her best friend's house consumed her spare time. When she married Bill, she moved into his suburban world. They lived in one of those neighborhoods with big houses on small lots. Mowing their lawn probably took ten minutes. We seldom saw her after the wedding, even on holidays. I barely knew my niece and nephew. I went to bed but spent an anxious, wakeful night.

On Saturday, I rose and checked my phone messages. Dad's attorney had called concerning the will. I made a note to cancel the reading of the will. No doubt there would be fees involved. My phone buzzed. Against my better judgment, I answered it.

"Mr. Harris, this is Nurse Matthews at the hospital. I've called to let you know your father has been moved out of intensive care."

"So I was informed yesterday when I called."

"Oh. Sorry, it's not in the records. Anyway, he's doing much better. You really have the most wonderful father. He has quite the personality."

"What? You mean he's able to speak?"

"He regained consciousness yesterday, and today he's been talking with the nurses. He's a remarkable man and a very lucky one."

I promised to come to the hospital but found myself unable to move. Instead, I called my sister. No answer. The phone was still in my hand when it buzzed with an incoming call.

"Mr. Harris, this is Dr. Hadley. We think your father may be able to come home by Monday."

"But Doctor, he was in intensive care a couple of days ago."

"He's made remarkable progress. Of course, it will take some time to determine his limits." Remarkable—the nurse had used that word. "He'll need assistance for at least a few weeks until he gets some of his strength back. Perhaps a nurse could be retained if you can't take off work."

It was too much to process. I showered, dressed, and drove to the hospital. After getting the room number at the information desk, I rode the elevator to the third floor with a sense of foreboding. I was relieved to find him asleep. The nurse's station confirmed his scheduled release for Monday. I didn't wait for him to wake up.

In the afternoon, I tried reaching my sister once more. She wasn't home, or more likely wasn't answering. Later, I went out for a hamburger. I spent the evening channel surfing without enjoyment. The restless evening turned into a restless night. I tossed and turned until falling asleep shortly before dawn.

Around ten o'clock I dragged myself from bed, had some coffee, and began to clear out my spare bedroom, which had, over time, evolved into a storage room. A few hours later, it still looked like a junk room, but at least there was space for a bed. I drove over to Dad's house and used his truck to move his bed to my apartment. I returned for some clothes and a couple of pairs of pajamas. That evening, I drank most of a bottle of wine before falling asleep, only to wake a short while later. The remainder of the night stretched out interminably.

I was awake when my alarm sounded. After showering and dressing, I remembered to call the office. It felt as though I had been away from work forever. Sawyer told me to not worry and to come in when I could, but he did not attempt to disguise the irritation in his voice.

At the hospital, I went directly to the nurse's station on Dad's floor and again confirmed he was due for release.

"Have a seat." The nurse gestured to a chair in the hallway. "He'll be ready shortly. We'll miss him around here. He has a lot of charm, you know."

But I didn't know. As a father he had been stern and disapproving. He almost never yelled, but I couldn't remember him ever exhibiting anything like "charm."

For about ten minutes, I waited. Then, down the corridor a nurse appeared, pushing a wheelchair. In it sat a hunched over figure, just the opposite of the tall, straight father I knew. The nurse approached, produced a sheaf of papers, and reeled off a long list of instructions. On the edge of my awareness, I sensed Dad staring up at me with a vacant, confused look. The nurse stepped away, and our eyes met.

"Hello, Dad," I managed to say. He continued to watch me without speaking. After a few awkward moments, the nurse returned.

"Once you get him home, he'll be back to his old self in no time," she said.

"No time" seemed like an eternity to me. I took charge of his wheelchair and the thick folder of papers. The nurse waited at the hospital entrance with him while I brought the car from the parking deck. Then Dad came home with me.

* * *

Six months later, Dad died. He spent his final months

watching television, seldom speaking. When he did, his speech usually consisted of "Turn the sound up" or "I'm hungry." I never saw the man who captivated the doctors and nurses at the hospital. Were they lying, or was it my inability to make contact with him? I never figured it out.

During those months, the sorting out of legal issues and other problems associated with my father's "resurrection" occupied much of my time. Although it strained my budget, I hired a nurse to care for Dad during my working hours. My sister never came to visit, though she did help with expenses. Liz stopped by a couple of times for short visits, but I could tell she was uneasy with both my father and me.

Dad and I never discussed our relationship. It was our last chance to resolve long-standing issues and come to some sort of understanding. I made a few halfhearted attempts to have a meaningful talk with him, but his eyes would glaze over, and sometimes he fell asleep. Once, when I asked him about his relationship with his own father, he knocked over a glass of water. Was it a purposeful act? I didn't know. In the end, it seemed better to forget the past than to analyze it.

Everyone told me how lucky I was to have this time with him. Many of my acquaintances and co-workers wished for an extra six months with their deceased loved ones. They envisioned a time of fond memories and expressions of affection. I couldn't bring myself to tell them it doesn't work like that.

Lydia

I wept for Lydia. At home I cried aloud. When out, I shed silent, internal tears. Her absence filled my thoughts and days. I wish I could say I loved her.

I first saw her on a crisp fall morning at the Epilogue Bookshop. The shop, a converted convenience store, boasted an interesting collection of used books and music CDs on its dusty shelves. That day, the local classical station played a string quartet from speakers set high above the self-help section. I stood in the literature aisle, thumbing through a copy of Stapledon's *Sirius*, recalling the aching sadness of that story.

When she walked in, heads turned. Only the clerk at the register and two other customers, all male, were present. To describe her features, one by one, would be to paint a portrait of many attractive women. What immediately set her apart was the way she carried herself. She projected a confidence, not born of beauty, but sprung from somewhere deep within.

She surveyed the shelves in her fine, white blouse and navy skirt, seemingly unconscious of the reactions she provoked, though surely she must have known. Each movement, however small, flowed with a natural grace, only increasing her appeal.

I had been content to watch her from afar, but she took me by surprise when she approached and began perusing the shelves a few feet from me. Her closeness seriously disturbed my own browsing. The likelihood of saying something inane dampened my desire to make a clever remark. I stood there, surrounded by great words, unable to summon a coherent sentence. She took a side step in my direction, and it broke the spell.

I eased around the corner, parked myself in front of the blues CDs, and plucked a Luther Allison disc off the shelf, pretending to check the track listing. Irrational anger stirred within me, first for not speaking to her and then for even considering it. Frustrated by my failure to act, I shuffled to the register with the CD and the book I had not intended to buy. As I pulled out my debit card, she appeared beside me.

"What's that piece of music?" she asked, smiling at the clerk and gesturing toward the speakers. He gave a surprised shrug.

"Borodin's second string quartet," I said, seizing my opportunity. She turned to me, and I followed up. "It's unusual in that the third movement is the slow one."

"It's lovely, isn't it?" She paused. "Are you a pessimist?"

"What?" Her question startled me. She nodded toward my book. That impressed me. Few read Stapledon these days. "Sometimes," I said, hoping it was the right answer.

"I know what you mean." She rewarded me with a smile.

The clerk tucked my receipt into the book and handed it to me along with the CD. With my business concluded, I found no excuse to linger. I took a slow step toward the door, and she turned away. My chance gone, I went out, silently berating myself. As I stood out front trying to decide what to do, she exited and glanced my way, offering an unexpected reprieve.

I approached. "Excuse me. May I interest you in some lunch?" She wrapped her right hand around her left and gave her wedding ring a slight twist. Though I felt certain she would turn me down, I persisted. "You can tell me what you think about Stapledon."

She eyed me thoughtfully. "Okay. Someplace not too crowded. My name's Lydia."

"I'm Ernest."

"All the time?" she asked. I laughed at the familiar joke.

We walked a couple blocks to an out-of-the-way Mexican café with bland food and cheap prices. We spoke of our shared affection for used book stores, with their musty smells and unpredictable collections. We were soon riffing on a wide range of favorite authors—a superficial, name-dropping conversation, though it laid the groundwork for finding our common interests. Emboldened by the easy banter, I invited her back to my apartment to listen to the Luther Allison CD. To my surprise, she accepted.

She followed my aging Chevrolet in her late-model Volvo. I kept checking the rearview mirror, unable to believe my luck. However, her wedding ring loomed large in my mind. Perhaps she had separated from her husband but continued to wear it, as some women do, to ward off unwanted advances.

I lived in the back half of a brick duplex, the last residence on a dead-end street. It was one of those streets severed by the freeway a decade ago. The space between my apartment and the freeway had grown into a thick tangle of weeds, bushes, and young trees struggling to escape the creeping kudzu. At least it blocked the sight of traffic, if not the sound. On the other side of the freeway the street continued, unaware of its missing half.

My shabby, messy apartment embarrassed me, though she seemed not to mind. I put on the music and sat beside her on the worn sofa, pretending to pay attention to the words but thinking only of her nearness. As the first track played, she leaned toward me and looked into my eyes. We kissed. Fumbling with zippers and buttons, we left a trail of clothes from the sofa to the bed. The next couple of hours passed in an intoxicating rush of awkwardness and pleasure. Then she had to go. We kissed at the front door.

"No one must know," she said. I gave a casual, understanding nod. She seized my shirt in her fist, drew me closer, and hardened her stare. "No one must know," she repeated, with gravity. "I have an eight-year-old son. He must not suffer for my actions. No one must know. It's my only request."

"Yes, of course," I said, trying, but failing, to match her intensity. She left, taking my cell number without leaving hers.

* * *

I worked from four to midnight, unloading semis at a home-improvement warehouse. The mindless job allowed time for contemplation. I kept telling myself that one day I would return to college and finish my degree, although I had little patience for structured education. My intellectual journey consisted of following my own curiosity. I learned a lot about many things, but missed out on the broad base of knowledge that college professes to offer.

Thoughts of Lydia eased the dreariness of my working hours, summoning up memories of sensual pleasure and shared passions for music and books. I wondered if I would see her again. She was too good to be true.

My phone chimed at nine-thirty the next morning. Twenty minutes later, she was in my bed. When noon approached, we got up and cobbled together lunch from the leftovers in my fridge. Afterwards, she explored my apartment, closely examining my book-shelves and music collection. Eventually, I steered her back to bed. We spent the rest of our time together talking, each still groping for a sense of the other, but we spoke only of the things we liked and not of ourselves.

Our meetings fell into a pattern, as all relationships do. She arrived around nine o'clock and stayed until noon, usually two or three times a week. In the begin-ning, lovemaking dominated the morning as we steadily expanded our range of sexual adventures. Later, conversations grew, moving with ease from the arts into social issues and politics. In those days every-thing seemed to be related. Soon we were finishing each other's sentences.

Each day I longed for the phone call, which would announce her visit. She always called. In the afternoons I spent hours in dreamy reflections of her presence. I took to jogging in an attempt to regain the trimness of my college days. I could do little to improve my apartment other than keeping it picked up and swept, however I cleaned out the refrigerator, a long overdue task.

Lydia rarely mentioned her son and steadfastly refused to talk about her husband, other than to say, "he travels." I didn't care to discuss my own stalled life, preferring to escape from it into her arms. The winter months passed in a blur of sexual and conversational bliss, the cold weather heightening the warmth we drew from each other's body.

When spring arrived, it brought a desire to be with her outside the cocoon of my apartment. I wanted to walk with her in the sun and bask in the envy of other men, but she feared being seen with me. She repeated her mantra, "No one must know." Undeterred, I proposed a day trip. Leaving at eight, we could make the two-hour drive to the capital, spend some time at the museum, go out for lunch, and return before school let out. Chances of running into anyone she knew were remote. She resisted, calling it too risky. Despite her reservations I persisted, and she finally consented.

We left around seven-thirty on a Wednesday morning. When we reached the interstate, she slid over next to me and rested her hand on my leg. For the first time, we were a real couple.

At the museum I took her hand. She instinctively withdrew it. I gave my best wounded look, and she surrendered to my unspoken request. As we roamed the galleries, she often released my hand to point out some aspect of the artwork before us. Each time I reclaimed the connection, although her ever-increasing reluctance diffused the pleasure of that contact.

She approached each new gallery with quick, nervous glances. My dream outing rapidly deteriorated. We cut our visit short and returned home without lunch. The trip back passed largely in silence. We spoke about the traffic and other mundane things. At my apartment, she gave me a kiss, got into her car, and left. Maybe our affair had run its course. In truth, it was hard to see where our relationship could go.

I went to work in the afternoon, hoping activity would dilute my disappointment, but the monotony of my job gave me too much freedom to think. Love should make one cheerful, positive, and outgoing. The secrecy of our affair suppressed those feelings, but did not temper the surge of excitement I felt each time she appeared at my door.

When she didn't call in the morning, I feared the worst. Our unlikely romance had no hope of a future. She never suggested she might leave her husband, and I couldn't compete with the security he offered. None of that prevented me from lamenting her absence. The urge to be with her grew throughout the day. I devised plans for reconnecting with her, each scenario more foolish than the previous. Finally I gave up, realizing the choice rested entirely with her. I tried to count myself as lucky to have had even a little time with her, yet my desire for more kept me from appreciating what I once had.

As I lay in bed a couple of mornings later, my phone chimed. Her number flashed on the display. She sounded as she always had. My hopes rose. I hastily showered and straightened up the apartment, which I had neglected since the museum trip.

She arrived looking as beautiful as ever, though a trace of weariness revealed itself in the corners of her eyes. We fell into bed immediately and made love with a hunger that left us both breathless. In the silence that followed, we each lost ourselves in our own thoughts. Finally she spoke.

"Ernest, I need some time."

"What do you mean?"

"I'm worn out. It's too hard living like this."

"You don't want to see me anymore?" I asked,

thinking only of myself.

"It's not that. You've been wonderful." It sounded like a goodbye. "I just need some time to recharge my batteries. It's just for a little while. I'll call when I can."

We made love again, slowly this time as if trying to wring every ounce of desire out of our bodies.

I stood at my front door long after her car disappeared down the street, thinking just how improbable our meeting had been. If, that day at the bookshop, she or I had arrived a couple of minutes later our paths may have never crossed. A contrary stoplight might have been enough. If the Borodin quartet hadn't been playing ... If Stapledon's book had not been in my hands ... There were so many ifs.

For several weeks, I went about my life. On the weekends, I went out to the bars with some of the guys from the warehouse. They were rowdy, fun-loving fellows, and I enjoyed being with people again. Those outings helped push Lydia from my mind, if only for a few hours. But soon I grew tired of their repetitive jokes and declined their invitations.

I set aside my hopes for her next phone call. She said she needed time, so I decided to give it to her. I took *Sirius* from the shelf and began to read. Stapledon's biologically engineered dog is a tragic figure, too advanced for his fellow canines, though physically inhibited from interacting on a par with humans. The novel transcends its philosophical underpinnings and social critiques and engages the reader with an intense, melancholy tale of unrequited love.

After *Sirius*, I reread the books Lydia and I had discussed. Many of the passages brought her voice back to me. As I read, I listened to the music we both loved, never tiring of the Borodin quartet. In this way, she continued to be a part of my life as the weeks turned into months.

* * *

One evening in late summer while taking my break at work, I picked up a newspaper in our staff room and by chance opened it to the obituary page and found her there. I read it several times before reality began to sink in. Voices of those around me receded, and in the solitude of my mind, anger grew. Her silence felt like a betrayal. The notice didn't give a cause of death but suggested donations to a cancer charity. She should have told me she was sick. I claimed a headache and left work early.

On the day of her memorial service, I drove to the funeral home, parked across the street, and watched the mourners file in. I wondered if any of them knew. It seemed unlikely, but she may have shared our secret with a close friend. Unable to think of a suitable narrative to explain my presence, I returned home. I would have to grieve alone—the cost of secrecy.

Later, I called the funeral home, identifying myself as a friend of the family and inquired about her burial site. "Cremated," they said. No opportunity for closure presented itself—no companion with whom I could seek solace, no grave at which to say goodbye. I sent a small check to the cancer charity—the only tribute I could muster.

In my isolation, grief opened the door of fickle speculation. Maybe our relationship hadn't been as special as I thought. It had been clear from the start she liked me, but what tipped it over into the affair that lasted for half a year?

And what of her illness? Did she know from the beginning? Regardless, why did she not find some way to tell me? I had so many questions, but she took all the answers with her.

I recalled her words that first day. "No one must know. It's my only request." But it wasn't true. She demanded much more. She asked me to forego a complete relationship, never sharing the mundane chores of daily life, never facing the difficult decisions all couples must work out together, and never spending a night sleeping in each other's arms. Without those experiences, how could one be certain of love?

To this day, I have no idea why she chose to come into my life. I counted it as luck rather than the romantic notion of fate. I told no one. It wasn't her only request, but I honored it as if it were.

Between Eleven and Midnight

When I answered the doorbell, she stood there in a pale green blouse, tight enough to show off her breasts but not so snug as to be obvious. Short skirt, too, but tastefully short. Her shoulder-length, silky red hair oscillated as if caressed by a breeze. I suddenly felt younger than my sixty-five years.

"Come in, Freddy."

"Thank you, Mr. Palmer."

"Craig. Call me Craig, please."

She stepped inside. "Thank you for agreeing to meet with me at this late hour."

"It's not so late." I glanced at my watch. "Just after eleven. This way to the living room."

"You have a very nice apartment." She approached the large picture window. "What a great view from up here."

"It's the greatest city in the world, but it's expensive. I keep an office here, so I can write off some of the cost as a business expense. Have a seat. Can I get you anything? I've just poured a glass of Cabernet for myself."

"No thank you, Mr. ... uh, Craig."

She slid onto the sofa and gracefully crossed her legs. I planted myself across from her in a matching armchair, admiring her finely toned calves. The short skirt had been an excellent choice. She leaned forward, demanding my attention.

"Let me get right to the point, Craig. I want you to

reconsider your casting decision. I believe I'm better than—"

"Better than Carol? That's great. You should always feel positive about your auditions. You'll never get anywhere if you lack confidence."

"I know the role. I know that character. I—"

"Whoa. Wait a minute. No one said you weren't talented. In fact, you were good, very good. With some hard work and a little luck, you might make it big."

"I'm good enough, now."

"You're probably right, Freddy. But Carol's got the gift, and she has stage experience. There were four or five actresses we could have chosen. It was a close call, but there was only one part. That's just the way the business is."

She leaned back with a sigh. She had ambition, talent, and looks—a formidable combination for a young actress. Twenty years ago, I would have seduced her with promises. I had done so with many others. Perhaps she might try to seduce me. Would her drive push her that far? Maybe. It would have to be her choice. At my age, I didn't want to see my name in a lurid headline.

"Are you sure you won't have a glass of wine?"

"Okay."

Clearly, she seized on the offer as an opportunity to extend our conversation. That was fine with me. Chatting with an attractive woman gave me pleasure even if we didn't end up in the sack. For many of my peers, the bedroom remained a high priority. I brought the wine and placed it on the coffee table between us.

"Who represents you?"

"The Flynn Agency."

"They're decent. They could be better, but they won't cheat you." I swirled the wine in my glass. "But if you get a break, find someone a little more aggressive."

"There's no chance?"

"Of what?"

"Of reconsidering the casting."

"Sorry, no. The offer's been made. It'd be a legal mess to rescind it. Besides, we're very comfortable with Carol."

"Is there some other play you can recommend for me?"

"Not right now, but I'll keep you in mind."

She raised the wine glass to her lips and then withdrew it. I allowed her the space to mull over her thoughts. What was she thinking? Did she consider the possibility of spending the night with me? I had no illusions. It would be an attempt at manipulation, but I wouldn't turn her down. Best to get her talking … put her at ease.

"So," I said. "Why are you pursuing an acting career? What drives you?"

She blinked and took a deep breath. "My mother wanted to act, but she never got further than a few local productions. I saw how badly she desired it."

"Be sure you're chasing your dreams, not hers."

"Oh, they're my dreams, too. Dad discouraged her. Beat her … sometimes." She seemed to drift into the past. "I withdrew into my own world where I could pretend to be someone else. I've always wanted to be someone else." She shook herself back to the present. "I guess that sounds like a cliché, but in my case it's true."

I shrugged. "Clichés often contain an element of

truth. Your folks still together?"

"They're not divorced, but Mom's in a home. She's got Alzheimer's. Dad lost his job at the plant. Now, he just drinks."

Why did the acting profession draw so many vulnerable women? Their desperation to succeed made them easy marks for power brokers in New York and Hollywood. Freddy had aroused my sympathy. She might make it if she was tough enough.

"That's rough. Any siblings?"

"An older brother. He joined the Army. Did a couple of tours in Iraq. He's in school on the GI Bill. He's struggling. I think he's got PTSD, though he won't admit it." She bit her lip and turned her head aside. After a few seconds, she continued. "When I make it big, I'll get better care for Mom and help my brother, too."

"And your dad?"

"I don't know how to help him. Not sure I want to." She sipped her wine, the glass still half full.

The mention of Iraq stirred a memory of my stint in Vietnam—a brutal, stupid war. My younger brother had served, too, but he didn't make it back. They never found his body. I still felt the loss ... if I allowed myself to think about it. When I was able to refocus, I saw not a young actress, but a woman with whom I had unexpectedly found a shared experience.

"Listen, Freddy." I sat my empty glass on the table. "I know Sidney Bruce out in Hollywood. He's producing a film that requires a large cast. There'll be lots of parts, though many will be small. If you want to go out there, I'll give you a recommendation."

She brightened. "Yes, definitely. I'll go. Thank you, Mr. Palmer ... uh, Craig."

"Don't thank me. You may end up as an extra or with only a line or two of dialogue. The competition is fierce. And a word of advice …"

"Yes?"

"Don't sleep with Sid. It's a dead end. Hollywood is littered with—"

"I get the picture."

It was time for her to go. She had what she came for. As I followed her to the door, watching the sensual undulation of her body, an acute awareness gnawed its way into my consciousness.

"Freddy?"

She turned. "Yes, Craig."

"Was any of it true? I mean about your parents and brother."

After a nearly subliminal pause, she replied, "Some … not much." She held my eyes with hers and lightly touched my shoulder. "You'll make that phone call anyway, won't you?" She knew the answer before she asked.

The door closed behind her, leaving me feeling magnanimous, yet unable to dismiss a tinge of regret. Why did I lust after every young actress whose path crossed mine? I shouldn't need to lay all of them. I'd had my share. There would be plenty of others willing to advance their careers in exchange for a night or two in my bed. What was the difference with Freddy? Was it that she actually had talent? Most of them didn't.

I poured another glass of Cabernet, put Coltrane on the stereo, and stood gazing out my window at the glimmering city below. Far down on the streets, headlights blinked like stars.

On an impulse, I picked up my phone and called

Brooke. She answered sleepily. I shouldn't have called so late. "Were you in bed?"

"Yeah ... What time is it?"

"Almost midnight."

"Everything okay?"

"Sure ... Just wanted to talk."

"You haven't called in ... God knows how long, and now you get me up at this hour?"

"I was thinking of you tonight and wanted to hear your voice. How are things?"

"Same as always. Look, Craig, I'm going back to bed. Call me tomorrow."

"You still with Jerry?"

"Yeah ... Call me tomorrow."

"Okay. Sorry to wake you."

I switched off the phone and stood at the window for a while, nursing my wine and listening to Coltrane's sax accompanied by the distant blare of a cabbie's horn and the melancholy wail of a siren.

An Easy Choice

That afternoon when I returned to my car, a scruffy, bearded man occupied the passenger seat. He wore a tattered coat and held a faded, red gym bag in his lap. A knapsack lay on the floorboard between his feet. I opened the driver's door and leaned in.

"Excuse me. I think you're in the wrong car."

He stared back with clear, blue eyes and slowly shook his head. I cursed silently to myself, remembering how often Emily had cautioned me about leaving the car unlocked.

I scanned the parking lot for a sign of the off-duty policeman the grocery frequently employed to discourage panhandlers. Shoppers hustled by, navigating around the remnants of a late-season snowfall, but I didn't see the cop. I left my bag of groceries on the driver's seat, walked around to the passenger side, and opened the door.

"Sir, you're going to have to get out of my car. I don't want to call the cops, but I will if you don't leave."

The faint trace of a smile tugged at the corners of his mouth. He appeared sober and didn't exude the unwashed scent of the homeless, though I wondered about his mental state. We faced each other in silence for a few moments. He seemed to take pleasure in our stalemate while my frustration grew.

"Sir, I'm going to call the cops." I brandished my cell phone but hesitated, unsure whether the situation qualified as a 911 emergency. He perceived my dilemma and flashed a mischievous grin.

"You don't recognize me, do you Michael?"

I eyed him closely. His voice dimly rang a bell, and I began to sense a vague familiarity.

His expression took on an ironic gleam, and he let me off the hook. "College hasn't been so long ago, has it?"

"Brian? Good God! Is it you? I didn't recognize ..." His appearance had changed dramatically. His ragged beard framed a lined, weathered face. Calloused hands suggested manual labor.

During our college years, we had spent a fair amount of time in each other's company. We even roomed together for a summer session five or six years ago. I had been drawn by his cutting wit, which didn't always hide his troubled psyche. When up, he was great fun, but when down, his moods turned dark and his humor cruel. He dropped out after that summer, and I had not heard from him since. I hoped time had mellowed him. His shabby appearance confirmed that prosperity had eluded him.

"How the hell are you?" I asked.

"I'm okay." He shrugged. "Saw you go in and thought I would surprise you."

"You certainly did. What are you doing these days?"

"Just got laid off at the warehouse. Planned on putting in an application here." He waved toward the grocery.

"I didn't know you were in town."

"Yeah, been here a couple of years."

By now I wanted to get rid of him despite a pang of guilt for not offering to help. "You should give me a call sometime. We can get together and rehash the good old days." I didn't really mean it.

He showed no signs of getting out of my car. I knew that strategy well. When down on his luck, which had been most of the time, he persisted in hanging around until someone, out of politeness, offered a meal, or a ride, or something.

"Look, Brian, I'm on my way home. Can I drop you somewhere?"

"I guess I can put in the application later."

"Where can I drop you?"

"I don't have any particular place to go."

I sighed with annoyance, but he didn't take the hint. It wasn't that he didn't get it. He simply refused to accept the social cues and body language of polite society. He habitually forced one to be blunt, often bordering on rudeness. The struggle had become uncomfortable.

"Okay. Why don't you have dinner with Emily and me? I can take you home afterwards."

I alerted Emily with a text message. We had been living together for three years, and she was seven months pregnant. We planned on marriage though had not set a date. She had completed her master's degree in education a year ago, but we decided to have a child before she took on a career. I taught at a small local college while trying to write the Great American Novel in my spare time. Teaching wasn't my dream job, but it had paid the bills while Emily finished grad school.

As we drove, Brian described a succession of jobs, the best of which had been managing a pizzeria. "The regional manager was a stupid asshole, so I quit," he said.

Whenever Brian failed, he blamed others, usually his immediate supervisors. Most of them probably were jerks, but on the other hand he never did anything to put himself in a position to improve his opportunities.

Despite his lack of success in life, he had acute observational skills and possessed a knack for honing in on a person's vulnerabilities. In college he used that talent to pick up women. At parties he scanned the room and, in short order, identified the most susceptible targets. Once he selected a likely quarry, he latched on. Through persistence and sharp wit, he often went home with her. His success produced a certain amount of envy in me and others, though our tastes in women were miles apart.

The two-story house Emily and I rented had begun to show its age. We liked its convenient location, but the rent wasn't cheap, and we struggled with expenses. I labored long evening hours on my novel, *A Question of Tenure*, a satire of life in academia. I had high hopes for it, but Emily had her doubts. Her criticism kept me grounded.

"Emily, we're here," I called out.

She yelled back, "I'm in the kitchen."

We found her tending a pot of spaghetti sauce, her protruding belly looking out of place on her otherwise slender body. We typically made large batches of spaghetti, chili, or something we could eat for days without having to cook again, though now we had to go easy on the spices for the baby's sake. She arched her back and gave a tired smile.

"Hello, Brian. Nice to meet you," she said, running her fingers through her short, dark hair.

"You two go on into the living room. I'll start the

pasta. We can eat soon."

Brian and I seated ourselves on the sofa. The memories began to flow.

"Remember the time a brawl broke out at the baseball game ..."

"The flat tire we had on River Road in the middle of the night ..."

"When we played football in the snow ..."

"And Lizzie Reynolds, God, she must have slept with every guy ..."

Brian laughed heartily, relishing each anecdote. I took pleasure in the memories, but years of grad school followed by full-time employment had reduced the significance of those undergrad experiences. I had moved on to a working life and the beginnings of a family. My thoughts looked to the future. For Brian, the college years dominated his half of our conversation.

"Why don't you go back and finish up?" I asked.

"It's all a bunch of shit. You've got to take courses that aren't relevant. I'm not going to be a scientist, so why do I need all that science? I don't want to learn a foreign language I'll never use. It's so fuckin' stupid."

"Sure. You'll never use some stuff, but it's what you have to do to get the degree. Everything in life comes with costs. You have to buckle down and get it done. It'll open doors for you."

Brian shook his head. "Buckle down ... Now you sound like my old man. He preached hard work, but it didn't pay off for him. After a while he quit trying."

Brian's father was a Methodist minister whose appointments consisted of tiny, remote parishes. I met the Reverend McKinney once—a short, white-haired man with a soft-spoken manner and a lack of personal charisma. No wonder his assignments had saddled him with smaller and smaller congregations.

"He didn't believe in God," Brian continued. "He just went through the motions for his paycheck."

I had heard it all before. Next, he complained about his mother, a rather strict elementary school teacher with no love for children. I wondered if the hypocrisy in his family life contributed to his cynical view of the world. By the time he finished high school, he was in full revolt. College only brought more authorities to rebel against.

At dinner I opened a bottle of inexpensive wine for Brian and myself. Emily shifted the talk toward motherhood. Brian made a few derisive comments about the difficulty of raising children, which I let pass. I evaded Emily's questioning glance and shifted the discussion to my novel in progress.

Brian had a quick and predictably cutting response. "Will anyone want to read that?"

"There's a lot of pretension in academia. I want to do what I can to expose it."

"And no one's done that before?" His eyes gleamed with malicious mischief. Emily smiled. She had posed that question on more than one occasion.

"Well … uh, the issue needs to be brought up from time to time. The subject doesn't have to be new if I can present it in a thoughtful, entertaining way."

"Who will read it?" asked Brian. "The ones that you're mocking? I doubt it."

"People like me will read it," I answered.

"Oh, the ones who are busy with a career and a family. They'll have time for it, right?"

That was quintessential Brian. His own failures must have seemed less damning when he could dismiss the ambitions of others. We had reached the tipping point in the conversation. My ego demanded that I refute him, imbuing my work with lofty notions of literary and social significance. That, of course, would provide further targets for him to shoot down. Things would escalate until I made some inane, indefensible comment. I knew enough to avoid that line, so I let it go. "We'll see what the publishers think."

I steered the conversation back to our college years. By eleven o'clock, I had consumed too much wine to take Brian home. He readily accepted our offer of the bed in our spare room where I did my writing. It had primarily served as a guest room when Emily's mother came for visits. In a couple of months, it would be transformed into a nursery. Unopened boxes of various baby products filled the closet, and a bassinet stood in one corner.

Later, in bed, Emily turned to me. "He'll leave in the morning, right?"

"Sure, I only offered one night. I'll drop him somewhere on my way to class."

"Where does he live?"

"He didn't say."

"You mean he wouldn't say. He avoided that every time. I wonder if he's homeless."

Emily's words forced me to confront my feelings. Considering the long lapse in our friendship, I couldn't say why Brian aroused my sympathy. There is something inexplicable about the bonds forged during those college years. I made a stab at easing Emily's fears.

"He's probably staying with someone, maybe sleeping on their couch. Don't worry. We'll be rid of him tomorrow."

I rose early and showered. Listening at the door of our spare room, I detected the muffled sounds of rhythmic snoring. Downstairs, Emily had settled at the kitchen table with her toast and orange juice. I poured a cup of coffee from the pot she had made for me.

"I don't think he's up yet," I said in response to the question in her eyes.

"Can't you get him up?"

"He'll never be ready in time. I've got to hustle to make my class."

"Dammit, Mike. Don't leave him here."

"Well ... he's not an early riser. In college he stayed up late and slept late."

"He's not in college now. I don't want him here, and you'll have the car."

"Listen, Emily, I just have the one class this morning. I'll be back before noon. Unless his habits have changed dramatically, he'll sleep until then anyway. Be nice to him if he gets up." Emily frowned and gave a dismissive wave.

In front of my students, I stumbled through a lecture on *Jude, the Obscure*. My heart wasn't in it. I had begun to consider myself a novelist, albeit an unpublished one, rather than a teacher. After class I brushed off a couple of inquisitive students and dashed home to find Emily curled up on the sofa, reading a child-rearing book.

"Thank God you're back." Her inflection conveyed relief with an edge of exasperation.

"I heard him get up, go to the bathroom, and right back to bed." Her tone hardened. "I'm ready to have the house to myself."

Upstairs, I gave a faint knock, waited a couple of

seconds, and then slowly opened the door.

"Brian," I whispered, giving a gentle push on his foot. He stirred and raised his head. "Time to get up." I backed out and closed the door.

In the living room, I gave a definitive nod to Emily. She ignored me and returned to her book. When we heard the hiss of the shower, she shot a sharp glance in my direction.

"Well ... it's okay. After he's done, I'll give him a lift to wherever he needs to go."

Twenty minutes later the shower stopped. By then, Emily had retired to our bedroom for a nap. Eventually, Brian made his appearance.

"Michael, do you think I could do a load of laundry before heading out?"

Though his request annoyed me, it seemed like a small favor for an old friend down on his luck. "Make it snappy," I said. "I've got a faculty meeting this afternoon at three."

Brian sorted his clothes and got the washer going. I seated myself at the desk in the spare room, booted up my laptop, and made an effort to get some work done. However, I lacked the necessary focus.

The blur of channel surfing drifted up the stairs. After a few minutes, music from the CD player replaced the TV audio. The rock-and-roll stirred my memories in a way Brian had not. It's funny how music can summon up the past. The familiar tunes drew me downstairs where I found Brian in the living room doing his best "air guitar" moves. He grinned and I mimicked his antics. We laughed at each other's awkward gyrations until Emily appeared in the doorway with a hand on her belly and a murderous scowl on her face. I turned down the volume.

"Sorry. We got carried away." She arched her back and said nothing before retreating upstairs.

"Okay, Brian, let's keep things down to a dull roar. She needs her rest."

He gave a shrug. "I guess you better go soothe your little woman." More than a trace of ridicule colored his words. His comment roused my male ego. I wanted to come to Emily's defense but stubbornly refused to let it show.

"She'll be okay. I don't have to hold her hand every time she gets upset."

Brian responded with raised eyebrows. Clearly he saw Emily as a high-maintenance woman with me as her submissive servant. Brian preferred younger women, less intelligent than him. They were easy to control, though he soon tired of them. He never sought equal partners, but I never criticized his choices. How dare he mock my committed relationship?

We listened to a few more songs before I made the excuse of having to use the bathroom. My face-saving fiction probably did not fool Brian. I felt angry with myself for allowing him to influence my behavior, but he had a way of getting under my skin.

In our bedroom, I put my arm around Emily's shoulder. She pulled away. "Get him the hell out of here," she hissed through clenched teeth. "Who's more important to you, him or me?"

"You, of course. He'll go as soon as his laundry's done."

She gave a disgusted snort and pulled a pillow over her head. I gently kissed her shoulder and eased away. Stopping by the bathroom, I gave the toilet a flush before rejoining Brian in the living room.

The washer and dryer took an eternity, but his laundry finally finished. Brian packed his things, and we departed. He directed me to a duplex apartment in a run-down neighborhood where he had been staying with someone he knew. We found the front door locked. Brian did not have a key.

I took him to campus, leaving him to roam while I attended the faculty meeting. After we adjourned, I spotted him in front of the library talking to Cynthia Wilkes, a freshman from my class. Cynthia had a history of emotional problems. She struggled with her studies and adapting to college life—just the sort of vulnerable woman Brian always sought. I barged into their conversation and coaxed Brian away, saving each of them from the other.

We returned to the duplex. A heavyset, bearded man in a black leather jacket and no shirt answered the doorbell. He glared at us through bloodshot eyes.

"What the fuck do you want, Brian?" he thundered. "I told you to get out and stay the hell away from Linda."

I tugged at Brian's sleeve. "Come on, let's go."

Brian brushed away my hand and persisted. "Aw, Steve, Linda's not my type, and I need a place to stay for just one more night."

Steve took a step forward. "What the fuck is wrong with Linda?" Anger bloated his reddening features. "You leave her the hell alone!"

"I just need a place tonight. I've got nowhere else to go."

Steve's eyes cut to me and then back to Brian. "What about your buddy here? Maybe he doesn't have a girlfriend for you to fuck with. Looks like a faggot to me."

"His girlfriend's pregnant—"

"You the father?" Steve interrupted. A sly, self-satisfied grin spread across his face.

I put my hand on Brian's arm. "Let's go."

Steve poked a finger toward Brian. "Yeah, go, you motherfuckers." The air felt hot with an acute threat of sudden violence.

"But …," began Brian.

Steve exploded with rage. Seemingly from out of nowhere, he produced a handgun. I backed away, pulling Brian with me. Steve took a couple of steps toward us.

I stumbled over a tricycle in the yard and fell sprawling on the sidewalk. Steve charged forward and aimed a kick in my direction. I rolled to avoid the blow which sent the tricycle tumbling end over end. An unintelligible curse bellowed from his throat.

Scrambling to my feet, I regretted that for once I had locked the car. I fumbled with my keys but managed to press the unlock button on the remote and lunge into the driver's seat. Brian had barely gotten in when I turned the key and hit the gas. The car shuddered as Steve landed a heavy kick against the rear fender. I kept my head low until we swerved around the corner.

It took several minutes for my pulse to resume its normal pace, but my anger with Brian remained palpable. He must have suspected we would get that kind of reception. How dare he drag me into that confrontation?

"Brian," I screamed. "What the hell are you doing, messing around with guys like that?"

"Steve's okay … most of the time. He's got it in his head that I'm after Linda."

I made an effort to dial back my anxiety. "Well, are you?"

"She's cute."

"That doesn't answer my question."

"Steve treats her like shit. She likes to talk to me about it."

That was vintage Brian. He often courted trouble by chasing after other guys' girlfriends. Was his obsession with women an attempt to find the love his family didn't provide? My layman's attempt at analyzing Brian no doubt oversimplified a complex problem.

"Well, Brian, what are you going to do?"

"I don't know. My sister in Springdale might put me up for a while, but that goddamn husband of hers is forever telling me what to do. I don't have the bus fare. I suppose I could hitchhike."

"Do you have things to get from Steve's apartment? Clothes or anything?"

"Got everything right here." He patted his knapsack and gym bag. "Michael, could I stay another night? I'll figure out something tomorrow."

I couldn't see how to refuse him. He had no other options. I didn't relish breaking the news to Emily. "Okay, just one more night. We need to start converting that room into a nursery."

Emily stared slack-jawed, her head cocked to one side, silently demanding an explanation. I recounted the events of our afternoon, leaving out the detail of the gun. She gave me the silent treatment until Brian went out "for a walk." It was as though he wanted to give us a chance to fight. Our discord would bring us down, closer to the level of his unsatisfactory relationships.

"We're having a baby, Mike. Don't you remember?" Emily stood with her hand on her belly as if to remind me. "I want to be sharing this experience with you, not with some derelict."

"He's not a derelict. He's a friend."

"That was a long time ago." She sat down on the sofa. "Now he's a damn nuisance. I wouldn't be surprised if he's on drugs."

"No, I don't think that's the case. He never got into that scene at school. Sure, we had a few beers and smoked a little pot. But he didn't like giving up control to anybody or anything, including drugs. Besides, he's never had enough money for that sort of thing."

"He probably steals."

"Well ... I've known him to do a little shoplifting at the grocery store when his money ran low, but he'd never steal from a person."

Her stress reached a shrill pitch. "My God, Mike, how many excuses are you going to make for him?"

I didn't want the argument to escalate. What made me so stubbornly defend him? I tried to embrace Emily, but she pulled away. When I persisted, she reluctantly gave in. I gently touched her belly.

"Don't worry. Tomorrow he'll hitchhike to his sister's, or I'll buy him a bus ticket myself and put it in his hands. One way or the other, he'll be gone."

Brian didn't show up for dinner despite a cold, drizzling rain. As much as he created problems by being present, he had a knack for being absent when expected. After dinner both Emily and I were restless, anticipating the tension his return would bring. The rain picked up. I found myself imagining him alone, huddled in a doorway somewhere, trying in vain to keep warm and dry. When Emily and I retired, we left the front door unlocked. Anxiety and guilt kept me awake. Deep in the night, I heard footsteps in the hall.

I awoke late and lay in bed listening to the steady drumming of the rain and the softness of Emily's breathing. Before I met her, I never considered having children. Now it felt like the most natural thing in the world. How lucky we were to have found so much in common, yet with enough differences to keep things interesting. I caressed her shoulder. She stirred but did not wake.

Desire for a cup of java roused me from my reverie. The aroma of freshly brewed coffee wafting up from downstairs surprised me, but a greater shock awaited in the kitchen. A slight girl, in a t-shirt and sweatpants, sipped coffee. I guessed her to be in her late teens.

"Good morning. I'm Annie." Her smile and cheerfulness exuded a familiarity that defied the circumstances. "You must be Michael. Brian told me about you."

I didn't try to hide to my surprise. "He didn't tell me about you."

"He couldn't have. We just met last night."

I was dumbfounded. "Mind if I have some coffee?" I asked with as much irony as I could muster. It sailed over her head.

"Sure, I made enough for everyone."

I poured a cup of coffee, excused myself, and withdrew to our bedroom. Emily woke at my touch and listened drowsily as I informed her of our new guest. She rolled back to her pillow with a yawn. "Wake me when they're gone." I returned to the kitchen.

"I hear your wife is pregnant." Annie bubbled with

enthusiasm. "How exciting. I want to have five or six children."

"With Brian?" I blurted.

"Too soon to tell," she chirped between sips of coffee. "But I want them to be smart ... like him. I think he'd make a good father, don't you?"

"Well, he's clever. Uh ... where do you live, Annie?"

"With my folks but I'm going to get a job and an apartment. Say, how much is rent for a place like this?"

I cited the cost, and her jaw dropped. "You should keep hunting for an apartment," I advised. "It's cheaper. Listen, Annie, what are your plans? For today, I mean."

"I don't know. The rain makes it hard to get around. I don't have a car or anything."

She veered off into a rambling appreciation of rainy days. While she mused, I thought of how quickly Brian would tire of her prattle. Emily saved me from further contemplation of the ill-fated romance.

"Good morning, you two. Having a nice chat?" she asked, from the doorway. Our new guest had aroused her curiosity.

"You're going to have a baby," squealed Annie, jumping up and throwing her arms around a startled Emily.

Emily managed to slip out of the embrace. "Yes, I'm aware."

I left them exchanging views of motherhood and got into the shower. Emily would have more patience with Annie than I did, but I tolerated Brian's intrusion more easily than she. Under the soothing warmth of the shower, I pondered the difference.

I had no classes, so I spent the morning at the

kitchen table going over notes for my novel. The plot had fallen into a series of clichés. I needed a dynamic event to enliven the narrative, but my invention flagged. In desperation I found myself considering a steamy sex scene to spice things up, though I abhorred the gratuitous coupling in contemporary fiction which so often brought the narrative to a dead halt.

The low murmur of conversation drifted in from the living room where Emily and Annie had apparently found common ground. When Annie decided to get a shower, Emily came in and sat across from me at the table. I shoved aside my notes. "What did you two find to talk about?"

"Oh, first one thing and then another. I'm trying to persuade her to get into a technical school or something. She's got a good heart but no skills."

"And no money with which to pursue more education," I countered.

"Maybe she can get some financial assistance. I don't have all the answers, Mike. I'm just trying to get her to consider options. She sure seems to live in the present."

"And Brian lives in the past. A fine couple they make. He'll lose interest in her if she exhibits any ambition."

"He's no good for her anyway," Emily replied. I shrugged. Our own problems were enough for me.

In the early afternoon, Brian finally roused himself. Emily and I were relaxing in the living room, dreamily listening to the rain. Annie had dozed off in a chair but woke, stifling a yawn as he entered.

"Good afternoon, Brian," I said. He grunted in response. "I can take you to the bus station when you get your stuff together. I called and there's a bus leaving for Springdale in a couple of hours. I'll stake you to a ticket."

"Going to my sister's is not a good idea."

"Somewhere else, then. I'll help you out."

"I don't know where to go."

"Don't you have some friends who can put you up for a while?"

"Not really. Only you ..."

My patience had expired. "Get real, Brian! I haven't heard from you since college." I lowered my voice. "I've helped you out for a couple of days, but this is a special time for Emily and me ... with the baby coming."

My anger must have stung. Again, I felt the stab of guilt. Emily and Annie braced for a confrontation. But Brian's face softened, his body sagged, and his eyes filled with resignation—a sensation he must have often experienced.

"I thought you might ... but I guess not." He retreated to his room and began to pack.

Emily turned to Annie. "What about you? You'll go back to your folks, right? Try to get in school somewhere?"

"I can't leave him. He needs someone. I can help him." I wondered if Emily's pregnancy had aroused the mothering instinct in Annie.

"Listen, Annie," I said. "He needs to get himself together first."

"That's right," came Brian's shout from upstairs. "Send everybody away from me." I hadn't realized he could hear. "I'm poison to the world," he yelled. He strode into the living room, continuing his tirade. "You fuckers with your complacency are so goddamn out of touch with the real world. Go ahead and write your pissy book no one will read. You've bought into all the fake comforts with your high-and-mighty attitudes. Go fuck yourselves."

He ripped the front door open and stormed out, leaving us to watch his receding figure in the downpour. For a heartbeat no one moved or spoke. Then Annie slowly rose, stood for a moment, and dashed out into the rain after him.

"Wait!" Emily called, but Annie never looked back.

Their abrupt and unpleasant departure left us drained. For the next few days, we went about our lives feeling a little stunned. The mix of guilt for not treating Brian with more generosity was tempered with anger for his intrusion into our lives.

Gradually, the joyous anticipation of parenthood vanquished all thoughts of Brian and Annie. Eight weeks later, Emily gave birth to our daughter, Katherine. She brought us much joy, though at the cost of many sleepless nights.

* * *

Five years later, my first novel, *An Easy Choice*, was published. I had scrapped my assault on academia, writing instead about a bright but troubled young man at war with the world around him. While not exactly a roman à clef, many of Brian's failings found their way into the personality of my principal character. As I couldn't imagine Brian getting his life in order, my protagonist descended into a deep depression with no viable options. His demons got the best of him, and suicide became an easy choice. It was not a recipe for commercial success, so sales were modest in spite of generally positive reviews. It did, however, enable me to land a faculty position at the university.

A couple of years after that, I ran into Annie near the campus. She was arguing with a policeman. I didn't recognize her at first, but an inflection in her speech caught my ear, and I made the connection. Using my clout as faculty, I interceded on her behalf, and the cop moved on. She looked a good deal older than her years.

"You working now?" I asked.

"Yeah. Waitressing at Sam's Diner."

"And Brian?"

"He ..." Her face fell, and her voice diminished. "Haven't you heard? We broke up ... and ... he died ... Took his own life."

Numbed for a moment, I couldn't speak. Then, "I didn't know." The initial shock gradually sunk in. Why had I not foreseen it? After all, my fictitious protagonist had predicted it.

I took Annie to a teller machine, withdrew two hundred dollars, and gave it to her. I hoped she would use it wisely but attached no conditions.

After dropping her off at the diner, I began to wonder if Brian had read my novel. Most likely he never knew about it. However, it was possible he had come across it. Could it have, in an improbable way, given him the impulse to end his life? Maybe it's egotistical to ascribe myself that much power over another person.

For a few weeks, I wrestled with guilt. How could I not? My success was based, in part, on Brian's miseries. I slowly came to terms with what I already knew. Brian's troubles had been deep and long preceded my acquaintance with him. In the end he would have reached his fate whether or not he ever read my book. I have come to accept Brian's choice as the only one which offered salvation from a life of despair. It had been easy for my fictional protagonist, but now that conceit rang hollow. How could it be easy ... for anyone?

Heartbreak Woman

I luxuriated in the cool sheets, soft mattress, and faint whisper of the morning breeze spinning the gauzy curtains into fluffy arabesques through the open French windows and dragging me back into a peaceful slumber to the gentle swoosh of the Mediterranean.

Joanie's rhythmic tapping on her laptop finally broke through. I raised up on one elbow and yawned. She sat naked at the desk, her slender, tanned body, long dark hair, and intense concentration giving contrast to the serene, opulent whiteness of our hotel room.

I rose with a stretch and kissed her lightly on top of her head. "I'm going to get a shower." She gave a barely perceptible nod, and I eased away, not wishing to disturb her.

The firm water pressure of the steamy shower invigorated me. I toweled off, desiring only a good cup of coffee to start the day off right. Wrapping the towel around my waist, I returned to the bedroom.

Joanie had risen from the desk and slipped on a robe. Her eyes focused sharply on me. I sensed an alarming change.

"You son of a bitch," she exploded.

I took a step back. "What?"

"You cheating bastard!"

"What are you talking about?"

"You heard me."

That was true, I heard her, but I didn't understand.

We had been together almost constantly since meeting a few weeks ago.

"Calm down." I spoke as rationally as I could manage. "Explain it to me."

"As if you didn't know."

"We've hardly been out of each other's sight."

"Apparently, it doesn't take long for you to—"

"Wait a minute. Tell me what you're talking about."

"That waitress you flirted with on Tuesday. Remember? I went out to meet my agent that evening."

I recalled the waitress—a cute young woman with an appealing smile and friendly manner, not unlike many of her profession. Perhaps I flirted a little. It was innocent and harmless. At least, I thought so. I hadn't seen her since.

"Where are you getting this?"

"Margaret saw you."

"Margaret … really? Your alleged friend Margaret, who I might add has a drinking problem, is your source? You said you loved me."

"I did until I learned the truth."

"Margaret's slurred accusations don't meet the definition of truth."

"Text messages don't slur."

"Hers probably do."

"She has photos."

"Bullshit. There are no photos."

"There, you've admitted it."

"What?"

"You said there're no photos of your cheating, but you aren't denying it anymore."

"Damn you. There're no photos because there's no cheating."

"Get out."

With no other option available, I threw on my clothes, gathered my few belongings, and slammed the door on the way out.

Down in the lobby, I approached the concierge. "Le taxi?"

"Oui, monsieur."

While waiting, I took out my phone and began the tedious process of searching for cheap airfare to the States.

"Monsieur?" The concierge held an envelope.

I accepted it and found an airline ticket to Atlanta enclosed. The taxi arrived before I could process my thoughts. Regardless of how I came by it, I couldn't afford to turn down a free flight home. On the ride to the airport, I mulled over the strange, unexpected confrontation.

Our brief romance had ended, but reasons eluded me. That airline ticket appeared so rapidly. Did she plan in advance on dispatching me? Maybe. Or perhaps her fame and wealth made it happen in short order. The rich knew how to get things done.

I began to question her mental state. After all, I'd only known her a short while. It takes longer than that to understand the multiple facets of anyone's personality. I suppose I could count myself lucky that her unstable nature revealed itself before I got more deeply entangled. On the flight home, I wrote a song about it.

* * *

A few months earlier, I had fallen into a funk and began to consider giving up my stalled attempt at a music career. I took a lot of pride in my guitar chops, but the bar scene in Atlanta was crowded with talented players. I jammed with many of them, though rising above the glut of Clapton wannabes proved difficult. Having recently turned thirty, I had begun to reconsider my career choices. Then the call came.

In the wee hours of a Sunday morning, I had just finished packing up after a poorly attended show at Hazard's when my phone chimed.

"Hey, man. You up?"

"Yeah, Franklin. Sorta. I'm done for tonight. I'm getting too old for these crappy bars."

"Listen, are you doing anything Saturday? My guitarist bailed on me and we're booked for a show. Can you help out?"

"I suppose. What's the gig?"

"A charity fundraiser ... for cancer. Starts early. Ends early. Easy money. Most of the well-heeled crowd will be more focused on mingling than listening to us." My bar gigs and succession of part-time day jobs didn't generate much income, so I accepted.

On Saturday, I joined Franklin and the Fantastics at an exclusive hotel on Peachtree Street. The ballroom, a crowded, cavernous venue, reverberated with lousy acoustics. My frustration simmered at the depths to which I had fallen.

While covering a Beatles tune, I let it rip, going off on an extended improv solo. A few in the crowd turned their heads, however most continued socializing. When we took our break, Franklin gave me an admiring glance and a thumbs-up.

I sought an exit door and stepped out into the warm southern night. The alley steamed with malodorous trash bins. I didn't see her until she touched my shoulder. Her smile obliterated the seedy surroundings.

"You play well." She positively shimmered, an angel in a glittering gown, missing only the halo.

"Thanks. I've been working at it for a long time."

"You working on an album?"

"No, I'm just filling in with these guys."

"I would love to have a drink with you later. We can talk about music."

She was drop-dead gorgeous and must have been in her early twenties. What did she want with a struggling guitar player? Probably not conversation about music.

"Sure. Sounds good." I was unattached. What could I lose?

She touched my hand and whispered. "My name's Joan Harrison. I'm in room 738."

Then, she vanished before I managed a response. She hadn't even asked my name. If not for the faint scent of her perfume lingering in the air, she might have been an illusion.

I returned to the stage for our second set. My playing suffered, as I scanned the room for her. Where was she? Franklin gave me a quizzical look when I failed to come in on cue a couple of times.

When the show concluded, I lugged my guitar case up to her room, unsure if her invitation had been real. I knocked. She opened the door, revealing an expansive suite and looking relaxed in a t-shirt and sweatpants. We started with wine and ended up in bed.

Afterwards, we lay entwined in silence. What was she thinking? Hell, I didn't know what I was thinking. Everything about the encounter felt unreal, but she had another surprise.

"I'm going to LA for a couple of weeks. Why don't you come?"

No commitments cluttered my calendar. "Okay. You're sure?"

"We'll have a lovely time."

And we did. She introduced me to movie stars and took me to the finest restaurants. We braved the horde of tourists at the Getty, where I got a firsthand glimpse of her fame. Despite dressing down and wearing sunglasses, she was recognized by several visitors, who requested autographs.

I knew she wrote novels. I hadn't heard of her, so I assumed most folks hadn't either. My mistake. An online search that night, while she showered, revealed a pair of highly acclaimed best sellers. Apparently, critics and readers credited her writing with insights into contemporary relationships.

Our stay in California stretched into a third week. Then she invited me to fly to the south of France. Heaven ... I had died and gone to heaven. The ease of our weeks together made her meltdown all the more baffling.

* * *

Back in Atlanta, I struggled to find answers. Struggled ... no, that wasn't the right word. "Failed" is more accurate. At first, I thought about it constantly, but the passage of time left me more puzzled than hurt.

An opportunity opened for me with Peach State Promotions, so I moved into the business aspect of the music industry, like many failed musicians before me.

It wasn't long before I met Karen and found my

true soulmate. We meshed in ways I never anticipated. Within a couple of years, we married. Our first child, a son, came along a year after that.

Through the years, I followed Joanie's career. It wasn't hard, the internet being what it is. She was everywhere, often with a new squeeze. Magazines, talk shows, and a role on a TV series. She had it all.

I read her books. One got made into a Hollywood movie. Ironically, her female protagonists always suffered at the hands of men, just the opposite of my experience. However, the bitter confrontations bore a fair amount of resemblance to our breakup spat. In her books, the men were always guilty.

Karen knew I followed Joanie's career. I'm not sure why I did. Rekindling our brief, ill-fated romance held no appeal. I suppose her celebrity status had a lot to do with it. That and her disconcerting pretext for ending our relationship. I didn't have the same fascination with any other ex-girlfriends, and Karen and my son gave my life a meaning that I could have never found with Joanie or anyone else.

When Joanie's latest book came out, the absurdly long title grabbed my attention, *A First-rate Affair with a Second-rate Guitarist*. I consumed the book in a couple of days. Two things offended me: the nearly verbatim duplication of our argument and "second-rate guitarist." On the other hand, "first-rate affair" appealed to my ego. Once again, her male antagonist proved to be a royal jerk. Why now, I wondered. She had been sitting on our story for the better part of a decade. The old questions came flooding back. The chorus of the song I wrote on that flight home leapt into my mind.

Heartbreak woman, she's so fine
Heartbreak woman, wastin' my time
Heartbreak woman, now we're through
Heartbreak woman, having someone new

On her official website, I lingered over the "contact" button. Should I express my resentment? After vacillating for a while, I let it go. Initiating an online confrontation might bring unwanted attention and disrupt my life. Besides, I suspected online contacts passed through an administrative assistant.

Another opportunity soon presented itself. Her website announced a book signing at an independent bookstore in an upscale mall in the Buckhead section of Atlanta.

When the day arrived, I took off early from work for a long-desired face-to-face reckoning. When I arrived, a considerable line already snaked around the kiosks dotting the main thoroughfare.

Cursing silently over my lack of foresight, I queued up behind a pair of middle-aged women. I did my best to block out their incessant babble. They droned on with complaints about the miseries in their lives. Judging from their fashionable apparel, money didn't seem to be the problem.

A man about my age, with a camera slung around his neck, stepped in behind me. He smiled and appeared eager to engage in conversation. I avoided eye contact and pretended to peruse my copy of Joanie's book.

The line began to move, albeit at a snail's pace. It took more than an hour before I caught a glimpse of Joanie, sitting at a little table. She looked great, as I both expected and hoped wasn't the case. Nicely but not extravagantly dressed, she exuded ease and charm as she conversed with each adoring fan.

I kept my head down while she signed books for the two chattering women. Finally, they moved on, and I stepped up.

I tried for irony. "Hi Miss Harrison, remember me, the guitar player."

"No, I don't believe so." She showed not a glint of recognition, an Oscar worthy performance. "How should I sign your book?"

I had envisioned a visceral response. Thinking fast, I said, "To a first-rate guitarist."

That produced no reaction either. She inscribed my book, handed it to me, and looked to the man behind me. When I didn't move, an attending assistant touched my elbow.

"Sir, don't hold up the line."

Confused, I shuffled out into the mall and plopped down on the nearest bench. I didn't know what I had expected, but the unsatisfying encounter wasn't it. The slow parade continued to inch into the bookstore and trickle out, each loyal fan glowing at their brush with celebrity.

Someone came and sat beside me, but I didn't look up. "You're the guitar player, aren't you?" The man with the camera held up a copy of Joanie's book and waved it with a flourish. I shook my head and hoped he would leave, but he persisted. "I couldn't help overhearing your exchange with Joan."

"None of your business, man."

"I dare say you're right about that, however we have something in common. Did you read *Photographic Evidence*?"

I had. Joanie's book vilified a photographer, who

first loved the heroine then did her wrong.

"You're Daniel?"

"Well, yeah, in the book. My real name's Denny Holden."

I introduced myself. "So, is it true?"

Denny gave a bemused grin. "What do you think?"

"Ah … She dumped you without cause, didn't she?"

"That's how I see it. Definitely not guilty of her charges. At least she's writing fiction and hiding our real names."

"Nobody would be interested in my name. I'm not famous. How about you?"

"People know my work. I'll bet you've seen some of my photos … the one of Joan with Lawrence Fuller at Le Chateau, lounging by the pool."

"That was yours? You're a paparazzi?"

"Paparazzo … singular. Occasionally. I make my living taking portraits of celebrities, though I'm not above snagging a few candid pics from time to time."

"You stalking Jo … uh, Miss Harrison?"

"Sorta. I don't bug her. I snap occasional photos. She seems to accept my presence. Are you stalking her?"

"No, but she still fascinates me. I wrote a song about her."

"Really? Let's hear it."

"This is hardly the place, but I can show you the lyrics on my phone." No one, not even Karen, had seen it. I wondered if I'd regret sharing it with a stranger, but our common experience overcame my reservetions. I opened the file and handed my phone to Denny.

He returned it a minute later. "Can you email this to me? Include the music with the lyrics. I'm doing a shoot in Nashville next week for Jason Hardtack. I know him fairly well. Your song might appeal to him."

"Uh … it's not a country song."

"That depends on how it's arranged."

After a moment of hesitation, I agreed. "Why does she do it, Denny? Why does she dispose of her lovers with phony accusations? I don't understand. Is it ego, or does she need that conflict for inspiration?"

Denny shook his head. "Beats the hell out of me. Analyzing her is way above my pay grade."

Six months later on a Saturday afternoon, my phone buzzed. Though the caller ID was unfamiliar, I answered anyway.

"Hey, it's Denny Holden."

"Hey, what's up?"

"Jason wants to record your tune."

I didn't have to think about it. "Yes, let's do it."

"Great. Get an entertainment lawyer to read the contract Jason's agent will send you."

"I know the drill. I'm in the business."

* * *

Jason's CMA award took me by surprise. The song, being in the country music genre, was never associated with Joanie. Other singers reached out to me for material, though I couldn't hope to replicate the success of "Heartbreak Woman."

A week or so later, I received a note in the mail, with no return address. It stated, in its entirety, "Great song. I do remember you." It was unsigned, but I knew. It gave me closure, a final parting gift.

Waiting for Adonis

I sit in the hotel lobby, watching the elevator. Every time the floor indicator stops at seven, my heart skips a beat. Will he get on? When it descends and the doors slide open, he isn't there. I pick at my sweater and smooth down the hem of my skirt. And I wait.

Brittany and Lindsay think I'm crazy. I can still hear them snickering in the back row of Mrs. Palmer's biology class. "You'll never get a glimpse of him," Brittany whispers. Lindsay pretends to faint. They're jealous. They don't have the nerve to skip school, but I don't care. It's the last semester of my senior year. Sure, I'll get a lecture from the principal, but he can't keep me from graduating. I've got my credits.

It doesn't matter what Brittany and Lindsay think. I'm not discouraged. I know I'll see him, but what can I say? "You're the greatest?" "I love your movies?" He's heard it a thousand times. I'm a nobody, and he's been seen in all the exclusive nightspots with the most beautiful women in the world. So I sit in the lobby, eyes glued to the elevator, just hoping to see him for a few seconds. It will be enough.

"I know who you're waiting for," says a voice at my side. A boy sits down on the sofa beside me. I give him a quick glance. He looks to be a couple of years older than me. I'm not impressed and return my attention to the elevator. "My name's Tim," he says. "What's yours?"

"Amanda," I mumble, immediately regretting it. I

sigh and hope he will go away. He doesn't take the hint.

"He won't come through the lobby. They have a special exit for celebrities. One day I'll be a celebrity."

"A celebrity what?" I ask, without looking at him.

"I'm an actor, too. Just supporting parts so far, but everyone says I have the makings of a leading man."

I turn and consider him. "You're not good-looking enough." I shift my gaze back to the elevator.

"I'm not so bad," he says. "Anyway, his good looks are mostly makeup and lighting. I'm better looking than him."

"In your dreams," I say.

"Why don't we go somewhere?" he asks.

"You go. I'll stay." The elevator stops on seven again, and I catch my breath.

"He's not going to be on it. Come with me. I'm rehearsing at a theater down the street."

"Go and rehearse." The elevator is descending. "You probably need it."

"You're wasting your time. You might as well come with me."

"I'd rather waste it here."

The elevator doors slide open and out strolls an attractive young woman, fashionably dressed, wearing dark sunglasses.

"See, that's his girlfriend, but he'll use the back stairs," the boy says. "I'm sure they've just finished making love."

"I don't think you're sure of anything."

"Come on, Amanda. My rehearsal will be more interesting than watching an elevator."

I turn and face him. "Bug off. I'm not interested in you or your rehearsal."

"Okay, okay. It's your loss. Here's my card if you change your mind. I'll jot down the address of the theater on the back." He forces it into my hand. "Why don't you give me your phone number? I'll call you later."

"Drop dead." His persistence annoys me. I'm relieved when he finally rises and heads toward the front door. He moves slowly as if giving me time to reconsider. No way.

I try to refocus on the elevator, but the spell is broken. I'm no longer confident the great star will appear. The boy has robbed me of my fantasy. I look around the crowded lobby. Everyone's going somewhere or doing something, except me. I feel a touch of sadness. The revolving door at the entrance admits waves of incoming guests. The boy might be waiting out front. I can't let him know I've given up. I decide to find the back door.

Adjacent to the front desk, a long hallway extends back. Down the corridor I go, past the restrooms, a custodial closet, and finally to the rear exit. Pushing through the door, I find myself in an alley. The trash cans, wooden pallets, and a broken chair are not unexpected, but surprisingly a taxi waits, its motor running.

Beside the cab stands a striking figure. The tall, thin man sports a royal blue shirt and pink overalls. Not real overalls for a working man, but silky, impractical ones. A fashion statement, I suppose. His spiked blond hair extends several inches above his head. He smokes a cigarette protruding from a long, narrow cigarette holder. I stare at him. He returns a casual, indifferent glance.

The exit door suddenly swings open again. There

is my idol, not in his cinematic glory, but dressed in an old coat and a worn-out baseball cap. Celebrity incognito. He doesn't see me.

The two men come together and hug. They kiss, laugh softly together, and fall into the back seat of the cab. The taxi revs its engine and speeds down the alley, stirring the odors rising from the overflowing trash cans.

Stunned, I stand there until a small object on the ground catches my attention. I pick it up. It's a pink button, torn from the overalls in the passionate embrace. I turn it over in my hand a couple of times then toss it away. It bounces and rolls for a short distance before falling on its side.

I stuff my hands into the pockets of my sweater and start toward the street. My fingers close around a thin object. It's the boy's card. "Tim Smith—Actor" it reads. His phone number and email address are printed there, and on the back, the scribbled address of the theater. I recall his face. He isn't a handsome boy, but he looks okay. A bit of a pompous ass, though. He might grow out of it. Some do. Perhaps one day he'll be a star. You can never tell. Should I go? The theater's only a few blocks away ...

Thanatopsis

I slipped into the chapel after the service began, like always. A knot of mourners, clustered together, occupied the first half-dozen rows. A couple of pews behind them a lone woman sat, her head bowed. I slid into my customary spot on the back row.

Despite the uncomfortable seating, I luxuriated in the hushed reverence only a funeral ritual can provide. The soft tones of the organ, the thickly scented flowers, and familiar rhythm of the eulogy colluded to yield a peaceful haven free from the clutter and chaos of daily life. My thoughts drifted along, touching on questions both profound and mundane. Though no revelations came, I felt my mind cleansed. Eventually, I turned my attention back to the podium.

The reverend droned on and on. The deceased sounded like a nice guy. They usually do. What a dilemma it must pose when the minister knows the recently departed was a royal shit. How many falsehoods are told out of politeness and decorum?

I listened for slips that would reveal the true nature of the "guest of honor." Generalities without specifics are the best clues. "He was a good family man" is one of my favorites, but when no examples follow, you can be sure something is being swept under the rug. Lies are for the living. The dead can't be hurt by the truth.

The proceedings fell into the usual religious framework, though in recent years I've noticed an increase in secular ceremonies. I wondered if the late Mr. Brown was a believer.

The program took an interesting direction when the musical selection turned out to be a recording of the second movement of Beethoven's Seventh Symphony. Was it a favorite of his, or chosen by a loved one? The aching sadness of the piece says more about the nature of death and grief than mere words can convey.

When the service concluded, I intended to make a swift getaway, but a loose shoelace caused me to stumble. An alert funeral home attendant seized my elbow, steered me to a chair, and bent down to retie the rebellious lace, all the while gazing at me with an air of practiced sympathy. By the time I escaped his benevolence, several black-clad mourners stood chatting in the foyer, blocking my path to the exit.

I shook a few hands, muttered vague words of sorrow, and edged past two couples already making plans for dinner. Finally I reached the door, stepped outside, and headed for the parking lot.

"Wait a minute," called a voice from behind. I turned. A petite woman with long, black hair approached. "Good service, don't you think?"

"Uh, I think … I mean yes."

"I could use a drink. How about you?"

I had counted on a quick departure, but something about her caused me to hesitate. It could have been her looks. Her dark, intense eyes, delicate features, and dusky Mediterranean tan compelled me to accept. I guessed her to be few years younger than me—in her late twenties, maybe.

"Come on. I'll drive." She gestured toward a late-model burgundy BMW. "My name's Olive, Olive Moretti."

"Matt Sinclair," I replied.

I watched her as she drove. Her elegant black dress whisked lightly on the seat. It looked expensive.

"So, Matt, how long did you know Tony?"

"Uh ... it's been quite a while," I lied.

"How long? You must have been pretty close at one time."

"Maybe fifteen or twenty years," I said, hoping she would cease the interrogation.

"You were childhood friends?"

"Uh, I guess I'm a little mixed up." Caught in my lie, I needed time to think. "It was a shock."

"Well, we're here." She steered the BMW into the parking lot of the El Salvador, an upscale bistro a few blocks from the funeral home.

The place was nearly deserted at three on a week-day afternoon. Only one other couple, having a late lunch, dined there. The hostess called Olive by name and showed us to a corner table. When the waiter approached, Olive waved off the menu and ordered a glass of Chardonnay. I nodded in agreement. When he withdrew, Olive narrowed her eyes.

"Don't lie to me, Matt. You didn't know him at all, did you?"

"Well, I do ... I mean, I did." I coughed and picked at the corner of my napkin. "Like I said, it's been a long time. What about you? How long did you know him?"

"Don't try to wriggle out of it, Matt. Look, you're caught, so you might as well admit it. I'm just curious. Why were you there? Come on. Confess. I won't out you."

Before I could answer the waiter arrived with our wine. A moment of silence passed until he retreated. I hoped the pause would deflect her questions, but her raised eyebrows insisted on a response.

"Well, I like funerals," I said slowly. "They're peaceful. I like to contemplate."

"Ha, that's a new one. You can 'contemplate' anywhere, anytime."

"Not me. The world's too loud. I like to get away from the noise. For my sanity, you know."

"You that close to going crazy, Matt?"

I laughed. "I guess not, but the serenity makes me feel better."

"There are other ways to feel better."

"I suppose."

"Like drinking." She raised her glass with a flourish.

"Oh, I don't drink much, just every now and then."

"Okay, but there are other vices."

In my mind, I ran through several possible vices involving Olive. "Yes, I know. So, what do you do?" I asked, in an effort to change the subject.

"Me? I do nothing. Not a damned thing. Angelo, my late husband, left me a bundle."

"Really? How did he come by his money?"

"His family had it, and he invested wisely. It's easy to make money if you've got it."

"How did he ... uh, die?" My question seemed to come of its own accord. I wanted to withdraw it, but she took it in stride.

"Heart attack, a few years ago. Too young."

"I'm sorry."

"Don't be. I'm over it." She checked her watch. "Look Matt, I've got to run. Give me your number, and

I'll call you sometime."

After she dropped me off at the funeral home, I sat in my car for several minutes replaying the odd encounter. An attractive woman with lots of money and time on her hands—that could be either heaven or hell.

As I headed home, I realized I had not offered condolences for … Come to think of it, I didn't know how she knew the deceased. Was he a relative or a friend? She had said nothing about herself, except she claimed to be a rich widow. She could be lying or exaggerating, but her BMW and fashionable dress backed up her words. Would she call? Maybe. She did ask for my phone number; I didn't force it on her.

Back at my townhouse apartment, I searched the internet for information on her, and came up with over four hundred thousand hits, mostly sites selling olive oil. I gave up and opened the market research questionnaire I had been creating. With the deadline still two weeks away, I had plenty of time. I made good progress for a couple of hours. Around six-thirty I decided to break for dinner. The doorbell rang.

"Hi, Barbara. Didn't expect to see you." She looked good, dressed in a green t-shirt and jeans.

"That's not much of a greeting, Matt."

"Oh, sorry. What can I do for you?"

"Just came by for a few things. There're a couple of boxes of my stuff upstairs in the closet. That is, if you haven't tossed them."

"Don't start, Barbara. They're still there. I haven't done much cleaning lately."

"What else is new?"

I held my tongue, knowing once begun the argument would escalate into a bitter, unpleasant scene, though I did manage an indifferent shrug. While she rummaged in the bedroom, I cobbled together a dinner of leftovers. Thank God for microwaves. Barbara reappeared with a small cardboard box in her arms as I was washing up. She gave me an insincere smile.

"Matt, could you be a darling and help me take the other box to the car?"

I lugged a large, unwieldy box down the stairs and deposited it in the trunk of her car.

"You'll need some help unloading that," I pointed out.

"That's okay. Todd will help me when I get home."

Todd had moved into her life as rapidly as she moved out of mine. It irritated me that she had landed a new man so soon. I wasn't ready to connect with anyone.

I hoped she had claimed all her possessions. Our romance had started well. I guess they all do. After a few years, the hours I spent working began to increase. I became more reflective and less outgoing while her social drive only seemed to grow stronger. I couldn't blame her, but our differences brought out the spite in her. The ending of a relationship is always sad, though we were better off apart. It was as much my fault as hers. Now that she had claimed the last of her belongings, I didn't expect to see her again.

I relegated Barbara to the past and spent my days working from home, thankful my job didn't require me to show up at the office. Commuting is such a hassle. After dinner, I stayed in, listening to music and reading. The solitude suited me. On a Wednesday, I attended another funeral. Thoughts of Olive came rushing back, crowding my mind, and preventing me from finding the serenity I sought. I looked for her among the mourners, half-expecting to see her there in her elegant black dress. She occupied my mind throughout the evening. I spent a restless night thinking of her. The following morning, as if summoned from my dreams, she called.

"Hello, Matt. It's Olive. How are you?"

"Okay." I paused, unsure of how to continue.

"I'm going to a funeral today. Do you want to come?"

"Well ... I don't know. Is it a relative or close friend? I wouldn't know what to say."

"For God sakes Matt, just go with me. I'll do the talking. You can nod and say 'I'm sorry' or something."

"Okay, I guess."

"Great. Give me your address, and I'll pick you up at two."

At the stroke of two, her burgundy BMW cruised into the lot. I watched her through the curtains. She surveyed the faded glory of the Greenwhistle Townhouse Apartments. The neatly compact rows had seen better days, though traces of an earlier elegance lingered. I met her at the front door.

"Hello, Matt. The service starts at two-thirty."

"Who's the ... uh, deceased?" I asked as we got in her car.

"Winifred Blakely."

I expected more information, so I followed up. "Was she a relative or friend?"

"Don't be dense. I didn't know her."

"Then how ... I mean, was she a friend of a friend, or something?"

Olive exhaled an exasperated sigh. "Look, I have

no idea who she was, other than what I read in her obituary. I go to funerals for the same reason you do. They're exciting."

"But I don't find them exciting. They're peaceful. Uh, you mean you go to random funerals?"

"Same as you. Don't you find the ephemeral line between life and death exhilarating? What could be more dramatic?"

I didn't know what to say. When she didn't continue, I sat back and wondered what I had gotten myself into. The boundary between life and death is a mystery, though I had never thought of it as "exhilarating." Perhaps it is momentarily compelling to one who is crossing over, but I preferred to put off thinking about it.

It took fifteen minutes to reach the funeral home. "Well, here we are," she said. "Let's go in and have a good time."

"We should wait until the service starts."

"That'll take all the fun out of it. Come on, we'll mingle."

She lost no time in approaching a fiftyish couple and introducing herself and me.

"I'm Mildred West," the woman said. "Winifred was my sister, and this is my husband, Edgar."

I shook Edgar's hand and nodded sympathetically to Mildred. At a loss for words, I turned to Olive, who leapt into the breach.

"Winifred's daughter, Suzy, was my partner when we were just out of college. I only liked girls until Matt straightened me out." She gave my arm a squeeze. Her inappropriate remarks horrified me, but not nearly so much as they appalled Mildred. She sputtered and coughed, reaching into her pocketbook for a handkerchief.

"Come, Olive. We should really speak to … uh, Mr. Jones." I took her arm and pulled her away, leaving Mildred wiping spittle from her chin.

"What the hell are you doing?" I whispered.

"I'm playing the game."

"What game? What are you talking about? And who the hell is Suzy?"

Olive knitted her brow and looked me over. "It's my game and my rules, but I'll take pity on you this time. Let's find a seat."

I tried to usher her into the back row, but she took my hand, led me down the aisle, and we squeezed into the fourth row among the family members. We acknowledged the puzzled looks with murmured expressions of sympathy. My uneasiness diminished when the service started, but my relief didn't last long. Olive began to sob loudly, attracting numerous side-long glances.

When the proceedings concluded, I hoped for a quick exit, but Olive had other ideas. I dragged her from a conversation where she was lecturing a bewildered couple on embalming techniques. We drove away with tears of laughter rolling down her face.

We ended up at the El Salvador. She bubbled with giddy delight until our wine arrived. After a couple of sips, she sobered up. A look of sadness crept over her face.

"I know you think I'm crazy," she said slowly. That may have been an understatement. "But I find the ritual so stimulating. It brings out the creativity in me, but there's always a letdown after it's over. I don't know what to do next." She swirled her wine glass absentmindedly.

"Was any of it true? I mean about Suzy. How did you know her name?"

"Don't be silly, Matt. It's all in the obit." She sighed. "Don't you research funerals before you go?"

"So, you didn't know Suzy?"

"Of course not. The obit said she lived in Australia, so I knew she wouldn't likely be here. I could have said anything about her. Did you see the expression on her aunt's face? It was priceless. Anyway, that old bag shouldn't have those prejudices these days." After a pause, she added wistfully, "I wish we could have stayed longer."

For a couple of minutes, she sat there gazing across the empty bistro, her eyes seeing something far away, and perhaps long ago. Finally, she regained her focus and downed the remainder of her wine.

"Want to see my place?" she asked.

Curiosity got the best of my better judgment.

We drove in silence. I can't say why I found Olive appealing. Her behavior disturbed me and disrupted the peace I sought. Her looks, of course, were a factor, and it felt good to have someone with whom I could share my odd habit of attending funerals. You can't find a woman like that every day. I told myself I could stop seeing her if things got too crazy.

Twenty minutes later, we wound through an exclusive neighborhood with massive homes on large lots. She punched in a security code at a gated driveway. Its path swung in a wide arc for fifty yards or so, lined on each side by a procession of stately oaks. The house, nestled among the trees, appeared to be of modest size at first, but when we got out of the car, I had to step back to take it in. The impressive two-story structure presented a neatly geometric facade of weathered brick. The gravel of the drive crunched softly beneath our feet. To say the grounds were well-kept would be an understatement. A young, dark-haired woman in a traditional maid's outfit met us in the foyer.

"Velma, this is Matt." She gave a quick curtsy, and I nodded in return. "Velma, bring a bottle of the Chardonnay up to my bedroom." It didn't take much imagination to see where things were headed.

Her spacious bedroom made the king-sized bed appear small. A large window ran the length of the room. The nearness of the trees gave the impression we were in an extravagant tree house. The tips of their branches scraped gently against the glass. The analogy of Tarzan and Jane flashed in my mind. My physique, while trim, failed to match that of cinematic Tarzans. However, the appearance of my "Jane" more than satisfied me.

The afternoon passed in a blissful blur of wine and sex. We threw ourselves into the lovemaking with abandon, leaving us both breathless. Afterwards, we dozed in each other's embrace. When I awoke, the sadness had come upon Olive again. She reached for me under the sheets, and we wrestled through another round.

I hadn't realized how much I missed sex after Barbara moved out. Our last few months together had been devoid of physical affections. Though Olive reawakened my desires, I didn't see how our affair could develop into a long-term relationship. For the time being I put my analysis on hold and decided to live in the moment. After all, I had no idea what Olive's ultimate designs were.

We fell into a pattern of meeting two or three times a week, always in the late mornings or early afternoons. I never stayed overnight. Whenever she called, I drove directly to her home armed with the security code for her gate, which changed weekly. Occasionally we attended funerals together. She clearly put more thought than me into which ones to attend.

In an effort to find common ground she toned down her outlandish antics, her "game" as she called it, and I tolerated some of her inappropriate remarks. Neither of us found complete satisfaction, but for a time we made it work. We both knew finding another who shared our peculiar interest would be difficult, if not impossible.

One morning a few weeks later, I lay in bed with Olive after an especially rowdy session. She buzzed Velma and ordered an early lunch. We had not arisen when Velma rolled the cart into the room. Olive slipped on a robe and dismissed her. I pulled on my trousers and joined her at the little table, which stood against the far wall. She nibbled at her sandwich without appetite.

Her mood lapsed into the usual funk that came on when no prospect for excitement presented itself. I felt an extra degree of fondness for her during these moments when I could comfort her with a touch or a hug.

It occurred to me our relationship had taken on some of the same issues I had with Barbara. Was the problem with me or the women I chose? I guess I didn't choose Olive; she picked me. Come to think of it, Barbara also chose me. Why was I so passive when it came to my love life? I resolved to think about it later. Olive broke my reverie with a nudge. A sparkle had returned to her eyes.

"Matt, it's time to spice up things a bit. We're in too much of a rut. Come with me."

With some trepidation, I followed her downstairs to a little room, which served as an office. She opened a door I assumed to be a closet. To my surprise, a long stairway led downward, ending in front of a heavy wooden door. She produced a key, and we entered a dark room. The soft, red glow of a digital alarm clock sitting on a shelf provided the only illumination. She locked the door behind us.

"What's this?" I whispered.

"Shhh ... I'll light a candle."

She stepped away, and a few seconds later candle-light flickered into existence, revealing a bare room. Olive returned to my side with the candle, took my hand, and led me to an alcove I had failed to notice. The recess was larger than it first appeared. There, on a raised platform, rested the largest coffin I had ever seen. Olive's delight in my astonishment was palpable. Her body positively vibrated with pleasure.

"It's not a real coffin." She lifted the lid and held the candle closer. "I had it specially made."

Inside lay a queen-sized mattress. She sat the candle on a nearby shelf and produced a short stepladder from a corner. Her robe slid to the floor, and she climbed in.

"Come on, Matt. Make love to me here."

My bewilderment rooted me to the floor until she called my name again. Slowly, as if in a trance, I removed my trousers and joined her. The lid slammed shut above us. I panicked and pushed upward. The lid refused to budge.

"Don't worry, it'll open again," Olive cooed. "You'll see."

"Show me now!" I gasped.

She laughed, and I heard a faint click. I pushed and it opened. Panting heavily, I tried to scramble out, but she held me tightly.

"Easy, Matt. It's okay. Calm down. It's a bed, like upstairs. We can leave it open if you wish. Come on. Love me. Play the game with me."

I allowed her to pull me back. My heart wasn't in it, but Olive applied her considerable skills to arouse me. We struggled through a laborious session. Her hunger bordered on desperation as I strove to please her.

Afterwards, she rested in my arms, her usual post-coital sadness absent for once. I lay there exhausted but unable to doze. My brain failed to sort out the multitude of thoughts and feelings radiating through my mind. Finally, she stirred and we rose. She kissed me with unusual tenderness, and I departed.

At home I tried to work, without success. I couldn't shake the image of that coffin in Olive's basement. I sat in front of my computer staring blankly at the screen. Nighttime brought no relief. Visions of being enclosed in a small, dark space haunted my thoughts. I lay awake until dawn.

Desperate for rest, I drove to the nearest drugstore and bought some sleeping pills. That did the trick. When I awoke around six that evening, I saw Olive had left a message on my phone. I didn't listen to it. After attempting to get some work done, I took another pill and went back to bed.

The strangeness of the encounter in Olive's basement unsettled me. Cutting off the relationship seemed like a good idea, but I couldn't bring myself to erase Olive's message. It lingered unheard on my phone and on the fringe of my consciousness.

On a Thursday, I trekked over to the mall to get a battery for my watch. While I stood at the counter someone tapped me on the shoulder.

"Oh, Barbara. I didn't see you."

"You must be losing it, Matt." She smiled sweetly and turned to the tall, ruggedly handsome man next to her. "This is Todd. Todd, my ... uh, ex."

"Good to meet you," he rumbled in a deep baritone. "Barbara's told me about you."

I wondered what that meant. And why the hell was he so handsome? And Barbara appeared to have lost some weight. She looked too damn fine.

"Seeing anyone, Matt?" she asked.

"Yeah." I hoped she wouldn't notice the tone of retaliation in my voice. "For a few weeks, now."

"Good for you. I wish you the best. We've got to dash. I hope there're no hard feelings. Okay?"

"Sure," I lied. "No hard feelings." Easy for her to say, walking around with a hunk like Todd. Maybe if she saw Olive, she would be jealous, too.

Normally I preferred solitude, but the encounter with Barbara left me feeling lonely. I found a seat at the food court and checked my phone. A second message from Olive had appeared. I overcame my reluctance and listened to them. The first asked if I wanted to attend a funeral. The date had passed. The other simply gave her phone number. When I got home, I gave her a call.

"Hi, Olive. It's Matt." Silence. For a moment, I thought my call had been dropped, or she had hung up.

"Well hey, Matt. I was afraid I'd scared you off. I've been missing you."

"I miss you, too." That wasn't exactly true, but it seemed like the best thing to say.

"Come over. We'll talk." She gave me the current gate code.

Velma answered the doorbell and silently led me to a sitting room on the first floor where Olive waited.

"Thanks, Velma," Olive said. "You may take the rest of the day off, and the weekend, too." Velma withdrew without a word. I don't think I ever heard her speak. "Sit down, Matt. I have things to tell you." I took a seat beside her and hoped some good answers were forthcoming. "You see, I'm not well, really. I'm in therapy." That seemed like a step in the right direction. "Before Angelo died, he cheated on me many times." I opened my mouth to express sympathy, but she shushed me and continued. "It was hard to take. But once he died, he couldn't reject me anymore, couldn't cheat on me, or lie to me. I like you, Matt. You're nice. You'd never cheat on me."

I hardly knew how to respond. She sat back while I processed it. Maybe I should have felt like running away, but her vulnerability aroused my pity. The desire to comfort her obliterated all other considerations. Perhaps I had the need to be needed.

"I think you should have told me about … uh, your issues, sooner, Olive."

"I know, but I thought you might have left me. I can see now you understand. You do, don't you?"

"I guess I partly understand."

"Make love to me again, Matt." Her voice quaked. "I want you."

"Where?" I asked, cautiously.

"Downstairs would be nice." Sadness and hope managed to coexist in her voice. "It'll be easier this time. It won't be such a surprise."

She had a point. The coffin wasn't really a coffin. It was a bed with a bizarre frame built around it. "Okay, as long as we keep the lid open."

"Sure, if that'll help. I'll go and freshen up a bit."

I strolled down to the little office and waited. Her framed wedding picture sat on the desk. She exuded happiness standing next to Angelo, a tall, handsome Italian with a neat little moustache. A rich good-looking man like him would have many opportunities to cheat. Olive must still have feelings for him, otherwise she would have rid herself of any reminders of her unfaithful husband. While I stood there, I heard Velma's steps in the hall and the faint sound of the back door.

Ten minutes later Olive appeared, looking relaxed, and wearing nothing but her robe. She reached for my belt buckle. "Take your clothes off here," she urged. She slipped off her robe, and we descended the staircase. Once inside her sanctuary, she locked the door behind us as before and lit a couple of candles. We climbed into the "coffin." When she started to close the lid, I stopped her and shook my head. She shrugged, left it open, and pulled me closer.

Our previous lovemaking had been vigorous affairs, but this time we found tenderness. Afterwards, she lay very still in my arms.

"You know, Matt, I could die happy right now."

I gave a little laugh. "You're not going to die."

"Yes I am."

"We all will one day, but not anytime soon."

"I will. You see, I took some pills."

"You don't mean it." Was she serious, or was she "playing her game?"

"You'll see in a few minutes. I'm getting sleepy. It's my endgame."

Suddenly I became aware that her body felt heavy against mine. I sat up, panic surging inside me. I grabbed her shoulders and shook.

"How many pills, Olive?" I barked. "How many pills?"

She smiled and closed her eyes. "Enough," she murmured.

I scrambled from the ersatz coffin and stumbled to the door. "Where's the key?" I shouted. "What have you done with the key?" I returned to Olive and slapped her face in an attempt to rouse her, but she gave a reflexive frown and didn't open her eyes.

The key had to be somewhere. The room was devoid of anything except a couple of candles, the coffin, and the clock. It shouldn't have been too hard to find the key. I searched under Olive's unmoving body and reached beneath the mattress where she may have hidden it. No luck. With a candle in hand, I crawled about the floor examining every inch of the surface. I checked the empty shelves, to no avail. Desperation seized me, and I repeated my search. One of the candles flickered and went out. The other grew short. Soon I would be in the dark, except for that damned clock.

I pounded on the door and yelled. Even if Velma came back, she couldn't hear me. The thick, wooden door and long staircase prevented communication with the outside world. I thought of my cell phone in my trousers, upstairs in the office. Perhaps when Velma returned and discovered Olive missing, a search would be conducted. Someone would find my clothes and eventually figure it out. But time was running short for Olive. She needed help. Even now it might be too late.

I approached the coffin. Olive's breathing had become faint. I climbed in and lay there holding her. It was all I could do. She expired shortly after the last candle burned out.

I got up and paced the floor, glancing occasionally at the clock. Was it there to torture me, counting the minutes of my life slipping away? I resisted the urge to unplug it, considering it provided the only light.

The air grew chilly, and I wished for my clothes. The coffin offered the warmest spot. At least there I could escape the cold floor, but I couldn't bring myself to get in with her. However, I did retrieve one of the pillows, curled up on it, and waited.

Did she mean to take me with her? I didn't think so, all evidence to the contrary. Hours passed. No sounds reached my ears. I began to contemplate the possibility of dying in that room.

Unexpectedly the alarm clock sounded. Its buzzing echoed loudly in the bare room. I moved to silence it, and my hand touched a small metallic object, which lay on its top. It was the key. Shaking with the prospect of escape, I hurried to the door and inserted the key. The lock turned. I felt weak with relief but managed to stagger up the stairs, dress, and drive away without considering consequences.

Upon arriving home, exhaustion overwhelmed me. I fell into bed and slept soundly. When I awoke, I groggily began to mull over my options. Getting mixed up in a sensational suicide was the last thing I wanted. I began to consider what would happen if I didn't call the police. It could be several days or longer before Velma realized Olive was missing. By then they might not be able to determine the date of death. But Velma would identify me as Olive's lover and DNA would confirm it. I could say that I left Olive alive and in good health, but lying didn't come easily to me. Sometimes I envied those who had a talent for it. If the cops placed me at the scene at the time of death, they might initiate a homicide investigation. I could claim shock and denial contributed to poor decision-making on my part. Would that be enough? I didn't know.

The more I thought about it, the harder it became to contact the police. I decided to keep quiet and hope I could explain things to the authorities when they came calling, which they surely would. Perhaps my plan wasn't moral, or even rational, but that was the path I chose.

It didn't take them long. Several days later, two police detectives showed up at my door, and asked me to accompany them to the station. Once there, panic set in, and I blurted out the whole story, leaving no sordid detail untold. They recorded everything, often glancing at each other with raised eyebrows and an occasional sly grin. At the conclusion of the interrogation, they informed me a suicide note had been found in her upstairs bedroom. They released me, and I never heard from them again.

A week later her obituary appeared in the newspaper, stating only that she died at home. Ironically, the announcement mentioned no funeral plans.

* * *

Barbara called about a year later. She and Todd had broken up. I patiently listened to her complaints and got the impression she wanted to rekindle our relationship. I wished her luck, but did not invite her back into my life.

I think about Olive all the time and the "game" she played. Did her suicide count as a win or a loss? I suppose she got what she desired, but I certainly didn't feel like a winner, even though she allowed me to escape her "endgame." Maybe there were no winners or losers. When you don't know the rules, how can you tell?

The Revivalists

I spent a wakeful night in an armchair by the bed, listening to Edgar's labored breathing. Shortly before dawn, a gurgle issued forth from deep in his throat and then silence. Only sixty-four. Too young. I murmured a hasty prayer over my husband's body. Time was precious. I woke Rebecca, who slept on the living room sofa. She knew, without a word, the moment had come. She gathered her materials, disappeared into the bedroom, and closed the door.

Rebecca had arrived a couple of days earlier, less than twenty-four hours after I called. Her youth surprised me. "Eighteen," she said, though she didn't look it. Her reserved manner and drab, gray dress shrouded her with the austere gravity of an Amish child. She made herself useful cooking, cleaning, and doing laundry. I hadn't expected her to take on the duties of a maid.

I lay on the sofa, trying to rest, knowing the journey ahead would be long. Unfamiliar scents wafted in from the bedroom. I tried not to think about it. The deal had been done. No going back. I put my faith in Rebecca.

Despite my weariness, sleep eluded me. Edgar's spirit still filled the house. I could almost see him sitting in his easy chair, radiating his calm, reassuring presence. But he wasn't there. I resisted the urge to go into the bedroom and gaze upon his familiar features. Interrupting Rebecca would not be wise.

I lapsed into recollections of the first time I saw Edgar and our first kiss, so many decades ago. If only I could turn the clock back and relive those days. He would want me to be practical, set aside the memories, and keep my mind on the task at hand.

Reluctantly I rose, shuffled into the kitchen, and gazed out the window. The sun had risen, its rays lightly brushing the fresh, green leaves of the pear tree. Spring promised to be glorious. But Edgar was dead.

"Mrs. Hamilton?" Rebecca stood in the doorway.

"Yes?"

"We're ready."

"Okay."

We opened the large oblong package, which came the day before, removed the stretcher, and took it to the bedroom. Edgar's expression of contentment gave me comfort as he lay with hands folded across his chest. He looked younger than he had in ages. The scarlet robe he now wore surprised me, but Rebecca stressed the importance of ritual. Strange scents still lingered, though I detected a whiff of rose petals.

We shifted Edgar onto the stretcher, carried him through the kitchen to the garage, and slid him in through the rear door of our van.

"Get your things." Rebecca's clear, focused eyes expected obedience.

I nodded and retrieved my suitcase from the closet. Rebecca recommended jeans, sweatshirts, and any other warm clothing I owned.

When I returned to the garage, Rebecca asked, "Do you have the money?"

"Yes."

"I'll drive first."

That suited me. The emotion of the difficult night left me drained. Driving required too much effort. I glanced at Rebecca. She showed no signs of fatigue. We reached the interstate within minutes and headed north. I drifted off before we crossed the Virginia line.

When I awoke, we had stalled in the perpetual morass of the DC bypass. The interstate spanned eight lanes, and it wasn't enough. Rebecca took it in stride. Getting stuck in traffic always frustrated me. Eventually, we crawled our way into Maryland. My thoughts drifted to memories of Edgar.

He was my only love. We met in high school where he preceded me by a grade. We dated for a year while I finished. The draft took him before we could be married. By a stroke of good fortune, or perhaps bureaucratic oversight, he never shipped out to Vietnam. We wed upon his discharge.

In the beginning, we struggled. Steady work eluded us. Finally, Edgar got a job with an exterminating company, and I found employment as a secretary in the high school from which we graduated. After five years of saving, we scraped up enough for Edgar to start his own company. Things got better. We were able to buy a house and have two kids—the American dream.

I suppose we didn't lead a dynamic life. We didn't desire excitement. The decades flew by. The kids grew up, married, and built lives of their own. Alan lived in Phoenix, and Cathy settled in Omaha. Though they produced four grandchildren, the expense of airfares limited visits to occasional Christmases.

After Baltimore, we stopped for gas and food. Rebecca surrendered the driving. When we hit the tolls, I appreciated her foresight in attaching an EZ Pass transponder to the windshield. Her silent efficiency and preparedness continued to impress me. She closed her eyes and slept while I negotiated the Jersey Turnpike. We crossed the Tappan Zee and pressed on into New England.

Keenly aware of Edgar on the stretcher behind me, I struggled to fight off the depths of grief and despair. Darkness fell, and we pulled over at a rest stop. Rebecca drew two apples from her backpack. I ate the one she offered, though I wasn't hungry. She took the wheel and our journey resumed. Traffic thinned as midnight approached, and in the tranquility of those early morning hours, I replayed the bitter events of the last two years.

Edgar's first heart attack came as a shock. The second cast a pall over our lives. Hopes for a long retirement together faded. Edgar fretted about leaving me alone. Our kids lived too far away to help, and over time the number of close friends dwindled. Most were beset with health concerns or financial problems of their own.

We had some savings but counted on working a few more years before retirement. When the business became too much for Edgar, he sold his company to a competitor, settling for less than he should have.

A year ago, Estelle Martin, my only close friend, told me about the New Dawn Community. I didn't believe a word of it. They claimed quick action could resuscitate the recently deceased, citing numerous medical cases when a person declared to be dead had been miraculously revived.

I checked the internet and verified instances on legitimate news websites, rare occasions when human error or undue haste led to a premature pronouncement of death. Those cases weren't true resurrections. However, New Dawn seized on them as proof of their beliefs. Only fools would fall for such a scam.

Several testimonies on New Dawn's webpage made extravagant claims. Dr. Peterson, a self-proclaimed expert on revivalist techniques, postulated that death had stages, and modern medicine only recognized the first stage. Prompt treatment, he said, could revive and restore the recently deceased. He put the success rate at seventy percent. It seemed like science fiction. As Edgar's health deteriorated, I pulled up the website again and spent hours desperately trying to justify their promises. Estelle reminded me that many religions disputed scientific "facts"—Scientologists, Mormons, Christian Scientists, and Southern Baptists among others. My own upbringing in the Greenfield Baptist Church emphasized faith over science.

Before his ability to communicate failed, Edgar expressed his wish to remain at home if possible. The hospice caregivers proved to be sympathetic and accommodating. I couldn't have managed without them. When the end neared, I called the number on New Dawn's website. I didn't want to regret leaving any possible avenue unexplored.

The woman who answered sounded reasonable—not crazy at all. She stressed that their procedures relied on proven, restorative treatments and not on mysticism. The cost shocked me, but I wasn't ready to let Edgar go. That seventy percent success rate began to sound like good odds. They promised to send a representative to assist and advise. Estelle sat with Edgar while I withdrew the money from our savings account.

* * *

In the predawn hours, we exited the interstate somewhere in Maine. When the road ended, we swung onto a narrow, dusty track. At a white mailbox with no number, we turned onto an extended, unpaved driveway. A light flickered in the distance.

We pulled up to a large, two-story farmhouse. An elderly woman in a robe waited at the front door. An overnight freeze had laid a frost on the land. I shivered as she ushered me into the house.

"Edgar ..." I began and gestured toward the van.

"It's okay. He'll be cared for. Sit down." Her severe, lined visage and clear, strong tone demanded compliance.

She steered me to the kitchen and into a chair. Rebecca had not come in. She must have been attending to Edgar. The woman put a bowl of hot oatmeal and a spoon in front of me.

"Eat, Mrs. Hamilton. Name's Lillian."

She sat across from me, without speaking, while I ate. When I finished, she led me upstairs to a room with two single beds. On one bed lay a thick nightgown. The frigid night rendered mine useless. If this passed for spring in New England, I wouldn't want to spend winter here. Once beneath the homemade quilt, exhaustion overwhelmed me, and I slept.

The morning sun through my window woke me yet failed to dispel the overnight chill. Thoughts of Edgar drove me to rise and slip on the bathrobe I found in the closet. I loved my husband. Waking without him by my side felt strange. Even here, far from home, I desired to make his breakfast and simply be with him while he sipped his coffee.

What would he think of New Dawn? I expect he would have wanted me to save our money for my needs. Now that I had to make the decisions, getting him back mattered more than our bank account.

Downstairs in the kitchen, Lillian and a young girl, about ten or eleven, were washing dishes. Lillian cast an expressionless glance in my direction and pointed to a chair.

"Lucy, scramble some eggs for Mrs. Hamilton."

I sat and held my questions. Lillian's somber persona imposed an aura of hushed reverence. Lucy cracked a couple of eggs into the skillet. Within a few minutes a plate of eggs and toast lay before me. Lillian brought a cup of coffee and seated herself at the table.

"Do you have the payment?"

"In my suitcase, upstairs."

"Dr. Peterson cannot promise results," she said, her voice harsh, her eyes hard. "There's always risk, same as in a hospital. It's science, not magic. Bring the payment when you're done with breakfast."

I nodded. "Where's Edgar?"

"He's under Dr. Peterson's care. The procedure may take several days. You can't rush these things." Lillian rose and resumed her domestic tasks.

After breakfast, I dressed in my jeans and thickest blouse. I pulled on a sweatshirt and brought the money to Lillian, which she accepted without counting.

"Lucy, show Mrs. Hamilton around."

The young girl dried her hands, gave me a smile, and glanced at my feet. She motioned for me to follow her to a closet where she produced a pair of too large hiking boots. I tied them tightly and stumbled outside with her.

"Take these." She held out a pair of gloves.

The midmorning sun had chased away the frost, though the air remained cool. Large, unkempt fields, sectioned off by a series of fences, surrounded the farmhouse. A few dozen sheep clustered near two women unloading bales of hay from a horse-drawn wagon. Next to the fields stood an old, weathered barn. A pale green, wood frame structure sat on a rise above the farm. Lucy made a sweeping gesture encompassing the landscape.

"It'll be nicer when spring gets here. The fields will have wildflowers. I love the Queen Anne's Lace. It's so elegant." She pointed to the building on the hill. "Dr. Peterson's lab is there."

We hiked across the field in the direction of the two women. They worked with a steady, comfortable rhythm. Lucy gave a shout as we approached.

"Hey, Tanya. Hey, Regina. This is Mrs. Hamilton."

"Good morning," I said.

The women nodded without pausing in their labors, pushing another bale off the wagon. Lucy shrugged off their lack of response and leaned close as we walked away.

"Tanya's the dark-haired one," she whispered. "And Regina's nearly bald under that cap she's wearing."

I wobbled over the uneven ground. "Are there any men here?"

"There's Tomas. He doesn't speak much English. He's foreign, you know. He lives in a cabin in the back pasture. Tanya's sweet on him. Lillian doesn't approve. Of course, there's Dr. Peterson. He has an apartment up at his lab. We seldom see him."

"Is anyone else here?"

"Just you. Sometimes Dr. Peterson has visitors. They don't stay long."

"Where are your parents, Lucy?"

"Dead." Her voice lacked emotion. "I barely remember them. Rebecca does, though."

"You're sisters?"

"Yes." After a reflective moment, she indicated a stand of birch. "Let's go there."

We entered the woods. It was as if we had stepped into the past. I imagined our ancestors stalking among the barren trees seeking a place to carve out a new civilization. The soggy ground sucked at our feet. The damp coldness wheedled its way beneath my clothes. It didn't slow Lucy. I would have loved it as a young girl, but my age and lack of regular exercise made it a struggle.

"Look here, Mrs. Hamilton." Lucy knelt by a fallen tree. "It's a sheep."

Rather, it was a sheep's skeleton, more or less. Though some bones had vanished, the ribs and a thigh bone remained. Lucy stroked the leg bone as if grieving. Should I be mourning Edgar or feeling impatient for his revival? The long trip and strangeness of the New Dawn Community had distracted me. Perhaps Lucy's job was to occupy me while Dr. Peterson plied his skills.

We picked our way along and happened upon a ravine, which cut a ten-foot-deep gash across our path. The stream running through it had not thawed. Lucy tossed a rock. It bounced once before getting caught in a frozen flotsam of decaying leaves. We skirted along the edge of the meandering ravine. I had no clue how to find our way home. Lucy knew. We came out of the forest behind the back pasture.

"Look, there's Tomas."

At the far edge of the field, a man wearing a wide-brimmed hat chopped firewood outside a little cabin. He attacked his chore with youthful energy.

"He's nice. You'll meet him later, but now, I have to get back. I have chores."

I trudged toward the farmhouse, trailing Lucy, with Edgar on my mind. Only Dr. Peterson could tell me what I wanted to hear. I desired to speak with him at the earliest opportunity.

As we rounded the house, a sheriff's car was just pulling away. It alarmed me. "Why's the sheriff here?"

"Oh, it's Deputy Bronson," Lucy said with more than a trace of boredom. "He comes from Stoneville. It's about the sheep. He thinks we're violating some silly local ordinance. Lillian always promises to do whatever he wants, but nothing ever changes."

Inside, I swapped the hiking boots for my slippers and settled in front of the comforting warmth of the hearth with my cell phone. "Out of service area," the screen flashed. I shouldn't have been surprised. New Dawn was in the middle of nowhere. Now that I had arrived, I wanted to let my kids know what I had done. Alan and Cathy would have tried to talk me out of it. They couldn't understand what it was like to lose a spouse. I wanted Edgar back even if it meant alienating my children. They'd thank me if the procedure succeeded. When Lillian passed through, I flagged her down.

"My phone doesn't work here." Her stare required me to be more explicit. "Is there a phone here I can use?"

"No. It's for incoming calls."

"But, I want ..."

She turned and walked into the kitchen. I followed her.

"When can I talk to Dr. Peterson?"

She began to inspect the contents of the cupboard and spoke while still perusing the shelves.

"You will receive notification when he has results."

I raised my voice. "I have to speak with him. Can I go up to his lab?"

"No. Visitors aren't allowed."

"It's not fair to keep me in the dark," I said, with as much force as I could muster. "I insist on seeing him. I paid your fee. That entitles me—"

Lillian turned and gave me a hard stare. Nobody wanted to talk to me, except Lucy. I retreated to the living room and spent the remainder of the morning crying before the hearth. Why couldn't Dr. Peterson take the time to update me? Had things not been going well? I wrestled with the dread of impending bad news.

Tomas came in just before noon. A tall, strapping fellow with blond hair and blue eyes, his smile projected the innocence of an overgrown kid. He paused when he saw my distress. I struggled to hold in the tears. He moved to the sofa, sat by my side, and took my hand. I couldn't understand his words, but they were soft and sympathetic. What was he doing here? His physique and youth exuded health. Was he merely dodging immigration authorities? His look questioned me.

I waved in the direction of Dr. Peterson's lab. "Edgar ..."

"Edgar," he repeated with a nod.

We sat together holding hands until Lucy called us

for lunch.

Lillian ladled vegetable soup from a large pot. Only Rebecca was absent. Dr. Peterson, I learned, took meals at his lab. Tanya and Tomas circumvented the silence, exchanging quick, furtive glances. I suspected Lillian didn't allow open displays of affection. There were no signs of alcohol. It must be taboo, too. That was okay. Edgar and I never understood its appeal. Lillian declined my offer to assist with cleanup. She and Lucy busied themselves at the sink while the others departed to resume their chores.

I wished for something to occupy my mind but found no books or reading material of any sort, not even a Bible. A television or radio would have been a help. Without distractions, my worries for Edgar became nearly unbearable.

Desperate for any sort of diversion, I walked to the end of the long driveway and around the fringes of the fields. My heart ached for Edgar. In our younger years, we often went for walks at a nearby state park. I could almost sense him beside me now. Once, I reached for his hand. Grasping only empty air, a pang of loneliness pierced my heart.

After arriving back at the house, I sat on the front steps and watched the sheep as the sun descended. The lengthening shadow of the house crept across the fields. I hoped I would not have to endure many more long, idle days.

Before dinner, Lucy invited me to walk with her down the driveway to check the mail. We passed Tanya, Regina, and Tomas repairing a fence. Lucy waved. Only Tomas returned her gesture. The mailbox was empty.

Lucy shrugged. "Too soon. We'll wait. Roger brings

the mail from Stoneville. He'll be along shortly." She kicked at a pebble in the driveway.

"How many people has Dr. Peterson revived?" I asked.

"I don't know. Some." She picked up the pebble and flung it across the road.

"And sometimes he can't?"

"Yeah. It depends. He revived Lillian and restored her health. That's why she stays."

"Really? And Tanya and the others?"

"No. They just work here. Regina has cancer. She's counting on Dr. Peterson to revive and restore her when the time comes. Oh, here's Roger."

The white van rolled to a stop, and the driver called out, "Hi, Lucy, here's your mail."

He handed her an armful of envelopes and drove off with a friendly wave. Though Lucy was proving to be my best source of information, I didn't press her for more. If she tired of my curiosity, she might be less forthcoming.

When we got back, Lillian summoned us for dinner. Once again, Rebecca was absent. The silence at the table seemed due as much to fatigue as house rules. Afterwards, Tanya, Regina, and Tomas went out to herd the sheep into the barn for the evening. When they returned, Lillian and Regina ascended to their bedrooms.

A few minutes later, Tanya and Tomas slipped out the back door. Lucy winked at me before turning in. With my options limited to anxiety or boredom, I headed to bed, hoping for sleep to provide an escape. Before drifting off, I heard coyotes yipping. The necessity of getting the sheep in for the night became clear.

I dreamed of Edgar lying silently beside me. Was

he alive or dead? I didn't touch him for fear of confirming the worst. Then he was gone. I awoke and cried until pain and weariness overtook me.

Late in the night, a knock on my door awakened me. I muttered a reply, and the door cracked open. Lillian entered with a lantern. Behind her, a young woman with a suitcase followed.

"You'll have to share." Lillian's harsh voice grated in the stillness of the night. She left the lantern on the floor and promptly exited, closing the door behind her.

"Sorry to disturb you," the woman whispered.

She undressed, slipped into her nightgown, and extinguished the lantern. I rolled over with my face to the wall but didn't sleep. Was the woman a client? Did she bring a loved one for revival? She must have been tired. Her light snoring soon began. I finally dropped off just before dawn.

A sound woke me. The morning sun streamed through the window. My new roommate stood awkwardly with her right arm halfway into the sleeve of a flannel shirt.

"Sorry, didn't mean to wake you." She pushed her other arm through the remaining sleeve and buttoned up. She wore jeans and hiking boots.

I sat up and summoned a smile. "My name's Judith Hamilton."

"I'm April, April Simmons."

"Nice to meet you."

"Likewise."

I had questions, though hardly knew how to broach the sensitive subject. Fortunately, she spoke first.

"Lillian tells me that Dr. Peterson is treating your husband."

"Yes, but I can't get more details. Everyone is so hushed-mouthed about the procedure. Uh ... is your husband ...?"

"It's me. My doctors give me six months. Tell me about things here."

"There's not much to say. Let's have some breakfast. I'm sure we're the last ones up."

After consuming bowls of oatmeal, I took April for a walk down the driveway. A hike in the woods required more effort than I was willing to exert, and without Lucy I feared getting lost. I told April how I discovered New Dawn and all I'd learned since arriving. When her turn came, she didn't have much to add.

"A friend told me about this place. It sounded farfetched, yet I began to pray for a miracle. I didn't care about the cost. It was worth a shot; I can afford it. Anyway, the hospital didn't offer any hope, so I called. Rebecca showed up the next day. Now that I'm here, it doesn't look like anything. That so-called lab doesn't look very modern." After a pause, she continued. "You say Dr. Peterson revived Lillian?"

"That's what Lucy told me."

It felt good to have someone with whom I could bond. I prattled on and on about Edgar and our life together, my hopes for revival, and fears it would fail. In the afternoon, we found two plastic deck chairs and set them outside facing the lab. Neither of us detected any activity. I don't know what we expected. After dinner, we retired early, like everyone else. April gave me a warm hug before slipping into bed.

The following day started out like the previous. In the late morning, April and I stood among the birch trees watching the members of the community go about their daily chores. Tanya, Regina, and Tomas steered the sheep through a gate from one field to another. Rebecca dumped something onto the compost pile while Lucy swept the front porch.

I couldn't bring myself to ask April about the details of her condition. If she wanted to tell me, she would. And I didn't feel right about continuing to unload my worries on her. She had enough to think about. Our conversation flagged until boredom spurred April into action.

"Let's help them."

"They don't want help. Lillian said ..."

"We'll help them anyway."

I followed April. She marched across the field and tried to shoo one of the sheep toward the gate. It spun away and trotted in the opposite direction. Tanya raced across the field, trying to cut off the animal. It swerved around her and headed for me. I waved my arms, but the creature didn't slow down. It brushed by, and I hit the ground. Tanya ran past, muttering under her breath. April reached me as I got to my feet.

She grinned. "That didn't work, did it?"

"I think Tanya's angry."

"Let her be angry. We meant well."

"You meant well. It wasn't my idea."

April stuck her tongue out at me. I laughed for the first time in weeks. She put her arm around me, and we made our way back to the house.

"Let's help out inside," I suggested.

"I'd rather chase sheep than sweep, but I guess you're right. We're out of our league when it comes to herding livestock."

We found a broom and dust cloth and threw ourselves into it. Lillian shot us a glare of disapproval. In my mind, I was doing it for Edgar, like at home. After lunch, we scrubbed down the cabinets and appliances in the kitchen. April attacked the tasks with a vigor belying her condition. By late afternoon, fatigue enveloped both of us.

After dinner, we sat on the front porch, despite the encroaching evening chill. The sun hung low in the sky. Somewhere in the distance a siren wailed, possibly an ambulance rushing to a traffic accident or the sheriff chasing a speeder. I shivered and rubbed my hands together for warmth.

"Let's call it a night, April. It's getting too cold for me."

When she didn't respond, I reached over and touched her arm. An expression of dismay had spread across her face.

"Dammit," she uttered with a frown.

For a few moments, I didn't detect the cause of her distress. Then I noticed the howling sirens growing louder. I followed her gaze. Three sheriff's cruisers barreled up the driveway, leaving a tsunami of dust in the twilight. The lead vehicle grated to a stop in front of us. Two officers sprang from the vehicle. The other cars roared past, climbing the hill to Dr. Peterson's lab.

"Dammit," April repeated.

"Inside, ladies," ordered the first officer. His partner followed. In the living room, Tomas leapt from his chair and dashed for the back door. Lillian entered from the kitchen.

"What do you want?" she demanded.

The deputy responded with a calm authority. "Everyone's under arrest."

"Fire!" The scream came from above. Tanya flew

down the stairs, stumbling and nearly falling. "The lab's on fire!"

Everyone hustled outside and ran up the hill where smoke poured from the far end of the lab.

"Edgar!" I shouted.

The deputies had bashed in the front door. I charged in after them. The smoke stung my eyes. Someone banged into me and I fell. I managed to pull myself up. An explosive, glassy pop sounded nearby— a window, perhaps. Flames leapt up around me. A voice nearby shouted, "Get out." I slipped and fell again. An arm wrapped around my waist and lifted me. We crashed into something and spun around. Then darkness and cool night air enveloped us. I lay on the hard ground, my eyes watering.

The brilliant light from the fire backlit the figure leaning over me. No mistaking the blurry face of Tomas.

"Edgar," I croaked.

He laid me on the ground. I think he reentered the building. A coughing fit shook me. I tried to stand, but could not rise. The fire raged and time passed, I'm not sure how much. A deputy found me and called for the medics.

I vaguely remember the ambulance ride to the hospital. I thought of Edgar. Did he get out? It happened so quickly. Maybe Tomas rescued him, too. At the hospital, a doctor examined me, and then a nurse guided me to a room and told me to wait. Later, she brought April in, looking sooty and disheveled. My appearance must have been similar.

"What about Edgar?" I asked. "Did he get out?"

"I don't think so, Judith. Everyone from the farm is okay, except Tomas. They can't locate him."

"Then they're dead—Edgar and Tomas. Tomas saved me. I think he went back for Edgar."

"Edgar was already dead, Judith. You brought him here because he was dead."

I had no response. Edgar ... gone, never to return. His body had been consumed by the fire. Tomas, too. Neither of us spoke for several minutes.

"Judith?"

"Yes?"

"Judith, I have a confession." I had no interest in her confession. "I must tell you something."

"Edgar's dead. What else do I need to know?"

"Judith ... I'm not sick. You see, I'm not who you think I am. I'm a reporter, just trying to get a story."

"What?"

"The New Dawn cult has been operating here for years. They've never revived anyone. They take your cash, and after a few days they pronounce their 'procedure' a failure, which they probably told you was a possibility. That gives them plausible deniability. Everyone's been arrested, except us and Tomas. They're searching for him."

I felt alone. April had gone from being a new friend to a lying stranger.

"Judith, I'm sorry. I couldn't tell you. I couldn't risk blowing my cover. New Dawn's victims have been unwilling to press charges or sue. They're afraid of appearing stupid in the media."

"You must think me a fool."

"No. Not you nor any of them. You're all vulnerable people, hurting and hoping for a miracle, but there are no miracles at New Dawn. My newspaper wanted to expose their fraud. I had to go undercover. I wanted to keep others from falling prey to their scheme."

"I don't want to hear any more." I wished she would just go away.

"Judith, let me help you. They'll release us shortly. I'll get us a room somewhere for tonight. We can't return to the farm until tomorrow at the earliest."

The room turned out to be in a cheap motel, the only lodging in the tiny hamlet of Stoneville. A shower relaxed me. I got back into my underclothes despite their smoky scent and slipped into bed. April had turned on the television. A crime drama played. I watched without interest. When the show ended, the local news followed. The raid on New Dawn was the lead story. April sighed, no doubt lamenting the loss of her scoop to the TV station.

On television, I saw Dr. Peterson for the first time. He had posted bail. From a wheelchair, he read a statement to the press, his long, white hair flowing down past his shoulders and his beard nearly reaching his waist. I had not imagined him to be so old. He spoke with a feeble whisper.

"We give hope to the hopeless. Is that a crime?"

"It is, if you can't deliver what you promised," a reporter responded. "That's fraud."

"We're in the business of gradual acceptance. It's a service to all who have lost a loved one."

The media peppered him with more questions, but he refused further comments. The news moved on to a controversy with the local school board.

April clicked off the television. "He's such a god-damn liar."

"What will happen now?" My energy level had sunk too low to express anger and disappointment.

"There'll be a trial, I guess. It'll last months, if not

longer. Let's get some sleep. We'll have lots of things to sort out tomorrow."

In the morning, a deputy drove April, Lucy, and me to the farm. Lucy had not been charged, due to her age. At Dr. Peterson's lab, a crew of fire investigators from Portland poked through the ashes, searching for evidence.

April and I went upstairs, changed, and began to pack our suitcases. Lucy came in and tugged at my sleeve. She pointed out the window, which over-looked the back field. I stared, not understanding what she wanted me to see. The sheep grazed there as usual, then it dawned on me.

"Who let the sheep out, Lucy? Were they out all night?"

She pointed again. Smoke curled from the chimney of Tomas's cabin.

"April, Tomas made it!" I cried with excitement. "We ... I must ask him about Edgar. Come on."

The three of us took a wide swing around the field and into the fringe of the woods, doing to our best to avoid drawing the attention of the firemen who seemed absorbed with their investigation. At the cabin, Lucy opened the door without knocking. Tomas sat in a chair with his head resting on a table. On a single bed in the corner lay Edgar. I knelt beside his body and cried with joy. Tomas raised his head and smiled.

That afternoon, I made arrangements to have Edgar sent home. I had not anticipated the legal issues regulating the transportation of a body, and the ex-pense surprised me. April offered to have her paper cover the cost in exchange for my story. I reluctantly agreed.

* * *

I gave Edgar a proper burial. Alan and Cathy came for the funeral. On their advice, I contacted a lawyer and filed a lawsuit in hopes of getting back some of my money. No longer able to afford living on my own, I moved in with Alan in Phoenix.

Justice was not swift. The New Dawn trials dragged on for years. In a stroke of macabre irony, Dr. Peterson died before the courts produced a verdict. In the end, nobody went to prison. They all got off with probation. Tomas eluded capture. The authorities probably considered him an unimportant cog in the scam.

The ensuing investigation revealed that a college student in Boston had managed New Dawn's website. He claimed ignorance of the illegal aspects of the operation, stating that it was simply a job for pay.

They never determined the cause of the fire. The government confiscated the land, sold it at auction, and distributed the proceeds among the victims. By the time I received my share, the money no longer mattered to me. My children will benefit when they come into their inheritance.

I will live out the remainder of my days in Phoenix, nearly two thousand miles from Edgar. I miss him, yet take some comfort in knowing that when my time comes, I will be buried beside him, together for eternity.

Sweet Jenny

I don't recall the first time I saw Jennifer McCullough, but I do remember when she first aroused my desire. On a bright Sunday morning, along with four or five other girls, she bounded up the back stairs at Northridge Baptist Church. She was a tall, lanky girl with an awkward gait, long, unruly blond hair, and a slight underbite. I had never given her a second thought, but that day she captivated me. Her lacy, white dress bounced as she skipped along. A white choker ribbon conspired with that suddenly appealing underbite to give her a delicate and undeniable allure. Our eyes meet briefly, and I felt sure she read my mind. I turned away, embarrassed by my transparent thoughts.

I must have been about fourteen and Jenny a couple of years younger. Previously, she had been an inconsequential figure on the fringes of my childhood, at church and at school, where she was in my sister's class. But from that fateful day onward, she occupied a prominent place in my developing libido.

On Sundays, she and her friends cut a lively path through the stern and sober faithful, attracting disapproving looks from adults and sinful thoughts from me. In that setting, I could gaze upon her without calling undue attention to myself.

Encountering her at school proved substantially more difficult. I was in my last year of middle school and she in her first—no chance of our classes coinciding, and lunches were staggered by grade. I caught an occasional glimpse of her boarding the bus. As the school year rushed toward conclusion, an unexpected opportunity arose.

"Chris," Mom said. "I have to chaperone Betsy's class on a bowling trip this Saturday. Graham's mother says you can spend the afternoon at their house."

Right away, my youthful and devious mind churned, wondering if Jenny would be among the invited.

"Uh ... Is the whole class going?" I asked.

"I think so. Her teacher said all the kids are excited."

"Can I go with you? I like bowling."

"Since when?" She frowned quizzically. "I barely got you to go with your class last year."

"I've been thinking about trying it again," I said hastily.

"I guess it'll be okay. We'll invite Graham, so you'll have someone to bowl with."

Bowling with the awkward, dim-witted Graham didn't appeal to me, though I swiftly agreed before some other option erased my chance.

Saturday arrived, and I found myself wedged in the back seat of Mom's car between Graham and beefy Cynthia Snodgrass, whose fat leg kept pressing against mine. Jenny and some of the other girls rode with their teacher, Mrs. Baxter, in her comfortable, spacious minivan. Several other vehicles hauled the remaining kids.

At the bowling alley, the sixth graders assaulted the shoe distribution clerk with screams and squeals while Mrs. Baxter and the other adults checked in and confirmed the reservations. Graham and I were assigned to lane twelve. I spotted Jenny a couple of lanes over with her usual gaggle of friends. On the lane between us, two couples argued loudly in a foreign language. Graham said they were Russians. I, however, picked up snatches of Spanish.

While Graham bowled, I stole glances at Jenny, who sported a pair of yellow shorts. I preferred to imagine her in the lacy dress she wore on that Sunday she first drew my attention. Each time I fixed the image in my mind, Graham nudged me to take my turn, or the feuding couples on the next lane exploded with a new outburst. To make matters worse, the uncoordinated Graham beat me by three pins. I wanted to slink home, unobserved.

My dreams of "Sweet Jenny" intensified, though I saw her less once I moved on to high school. At a church picnic following my freshman year, an opportunity to impress her presented itself. In an impromptu soccer game, I scored three goals. Among the cheering spectators, I spied Jenny and her friends jumping up and down. Afterwards, my parents drove home with Betsy and me in the back seat. She leaned over and whispered.

"I think Jenny McCullough likes you."

I welcomed the news, but the next step eluded me. However, I didn't let on. "Yes, I know," I said, speaking with exaggerated authority.

Betsy leaned back and stared at me with wonder in her eyes. "How do you know?" she asked, obviously desiring the ability to know such things for herself.

"One day you'll understand," I said with all the aloofness I could muster.

Fortunately, we pulled into our driveway before Betsy could demand a full explanation. I avoided her for the next few days, hoping she'd soon forget.

At school, most of the guys talked about girls, speculating about who would and who wouldn't. During lunch period I often stood by the entrance to the science building with some of the older boys to watch girls go by.

"There goes Alice Whisnet," noted Billy Strayhorn. "Biggest knockers in school."

No one disagreed. Her development obviously preceded that of her classmates. To make it even more apparent, she moved past us with chest thrust forward, pretending not to notice our attention.

"Wow," came a comment from behind me.

"Yeah," said Billy. "I had her once." A murmur of disbelief rippled through the group. Billy turned and in a cool, detached manner described Alice's anatomy to a degree that convinced me and some of the others, though most remained skeptical.

"Only once? Why not again?" someone challenged.

"Once was enough," Billy calmly explained. "She wasn't all that good."

"With a body like that, she's gotta be good," someone else countered.

Billy sighed and rolled his eyes. Then Lisa McMann strolled by.

"Hey Chris, you like that?" Billy asked, in a transparent attempt to cut short his own interrogation.

I cringed, fearing any answer would expose my inexperience. Failing to respond was not an option either.

"I ... uh ... yeah."

"You don't sound too certain, Chris," came a voice from the crowd. "You're not a fag, are you?" Laughter followed, and I reddened.

Fortunately, Sondra Jones happened by in a very short skirt. She drew everyone's attention and our fantasies followed. I breathed a sigh of relief and stole away. For the next week, I avoided Billy and his friends.

Anxiety filled my days and nights. The only cure would be getting laid by someone ... anyone. In my dreams it was always Jenny, but two long years separated her from entry into high school.

I soon learned to slip away whenever the group conversation turned to sex. I spent more time with Graham until I began to fear his dullness would rub off on me. After that, I retreated into the fantasy world of video games. My parents whispered phrases like "just a phase he's going through" or "he'll grow out of it."

The following year, my parents allowed Betsy to have her birthday party at our home. I feverishly hoped Jenny would be attending.

"Who's coming to Betsy's party?" I asked Mom one Saturday afternoon while she sat at the dining room table going over the arrangements.

"Most of her friends from school," she answered. "A few of the girls from church will be here, too."

"Think they'll all show up?" I asked.

"I just told you. Most of them, I guess. We'll see." She turned back to her plans. "Now go do your homework, and let me work on organizing things."

Giddy with hope, I set thoughts of homework aside, took my bike from the garage, and sailed off down the street. The rush of wind in my face and the exhilaration of possibly seeing Jenny in my own house sent me soaring around the neighborhood, before a sudden onslaught of worries brought me to a halt.

Maybe she wouldn't show up. Mom gave no guarantee all Betsy's friends would attend. Jenny was popular. Perhaps she had other plans. What if she had a boyfriend already? I dismissed that thought. She liked me. Betsy had said so last year at the picnic. Surely Jenny dreamed about me, just as I dreamed about her. Still, I could not be certain she'd attend. I pedaled slowly back to the house, wavering between elation and despair. The two weeks until the party seemed an eternity.

A couple of days later, Betsy plopped down on the sofa beside me. I shot her a glance and returned my attention to the video game I was playing. It wasn't like her to seek me out. I wondered what she had on her mind.

"Chris," she said. I took her tone to be mischievous but paused the game and looked at her. "Guess who's coming to my party?" she asked slyly. I suspected she meant Greg Strayhorn, Billy's younger brother. She had a crush on him.

"Beats me," I responded. "All of your bratty friends, I guess."

"Humph ...," she grunted. "Well, if you don't want to know, I just won't tell you."

Heaving a big sigh, I played along for the sake of household harmony. "Okay, who's coming?"

"Jenny McCollough," she said, gauging my reaction through devious eyes.

I must have flinched but tried not to show it. "Oh, her," I said as calmly as I could.

"You still like her, don't you?"

"Never said I did."

"But you do, don't you?"

"She's all right, I guess."

"Well, she likes you. She told me."

"That so?"

"Yes, and I told you that last year after the picnic, you dummy. Don't you remember? I think she'd let you kiss her."

"What do you know about kissing? You haven't kissed anyone."

"Yes, I have."

"Who?" I asked. "What moron have you been kissing?"

"Greg."

She stated it with such a lack of guile, I knew it to be true. I felt ashamed ... ashamed my little sister had a love life, and I didn't. "Go away," I said, flushing with anger and embarrassment. "I don't want to know about it."

She gave me a goofy grin and refused to budge. I suppressed the urge to strike her, threw down the gaming remote, and stomped upstairs to my room. Things had gone from bad to abysmal. All the guys at school talked about sex as if they were God's gift to the female gender. Though I didn't believe half their stories, it didn't matter. The sheer fact they had the confidence to spin their tall tales pushed me further and further down the social scale. To make matters worse, Betsy was swapping germs with Greg Strayhorn.

Over the next couple of weeks, I loitered on the fringes of Billy's gang at lunchtime. I hoped to pick up some tips on how to initiate kissing. Funny how the conversations always skipped kissing and went straight into the explicit details of various sex acts. I'd be on my own should an opportunity present itself.

Finally, the big day arrived. I awoke early and

made myself unusually helpful with the party prep-arations, drawing astounded looks from Mom and a knowing smirk from Betsy. A stroke of good fortune occurred a few days earlier when our cat, Sasha, gave birth to three kittens. She and her brood occupied a cardboard box in our tool shed. If only I could interest Jenny in seeing the kittens, without attracting an entourage of her friends.

The kids began to arrive, slowly at first and then in waves. I didn't see Jenny come in, but suddenly there she was, in the midst of a half-dozen giggling girls. As if my desires were known to her, she wore a white, lacy dress and white choker ribbon. I stumbled about, helping Mom and the other chaperones, but "Sweet Jenny" totally occupied my thoughts. Speaking with her amid the chaos and din of a houseful of thirteen-year-olds proved to be an unattainable goal. They roared through a series of games and a messy feast of cake and ice cream in our backyard. Eventually dark-ness fell, and the exhausted adults herded them inside for a movie.

"Chris," Mom called, "would you start cleaning up the backyard? I've got to get off my feet." It always amazed me how quickly adults tired.

I trudged out back and began to clear the picnic table of paper plates and abandoned party favors. The floodlight at the corner of our house cast its harsh glare over the yard. Faint sounds of squeals and laughter drifted from the house out into the night. A sense of loneliness descended upon me.

I heard the back door and glanced over my shoul-der, expecting Mom. To my surprise Jenny emerged, stepping gingerly through the scattered debris. The floodlight lit her golden hair and white dress. An angel, I thought.

"It's a mess," she said, stopping a couple feet in front of me. Thankfully she spoke first. I don't think I had it in me to be coherent without a little help.

"Yeah," I responded, sure she could hear my heart thumping.

"Betsy's lucky to have such a good big brother." Jenny smiled and surveyed the melting mounds of ice cream dripping through the seams of the picnic table. "I've got two younger sisters."

A different Jenny stood before me, not the one who ran and giggled with her friends—a quieter, more serious girl. I didn't know what to say, though I had to try something. "Yeah, I'm in tenth grade."

"I'll be in high school next year."

"Yeah, I know. I'm thinking of trying out for the football team in the fall." God knows it wasn't true, but that's what came out. If she doubted me, she didn't let on. "Hey," I said. "Our cat just had kittens. Want to see them?"

"Yes, I'd like that. They won't miss me. Your mom has turned out the lights in the family room for the movie." She cast a glance over her shoulder before looking back at me. "We have a dog, but I like cats, too."

I held the shed door for her and reached for the flashlight we kept on the shelf just inside. The fading battery enabled us to see well enough to keep from colliding with the lawn mower. We knelt together by the cardboard box in the corner.

Sasha blinked at us with feline annoyance. Two kittens snuggled by her side while the third mewed softly, searching for its mother's teat.

"They're so cute," breathed Jenny, close to my ear.

"They'll be even cuter when their eyes are open. We'll probably have to give them away. Want one?"

"I guess not. I mean, we've got the dog and ..."

Jenny's voice trailed away, and we rose. She stood close. I switched the flashlight off, leaned forward, and kissed her on the cheek. When she didn't turn away, I moved in for another. In the darkness our lips met. Relief rushed through my mind. Now I could talk about kissing a girl. We parted and then came together once more.

But kissing wasn't enough. The guys would merely laugh. If only I could boast of a conquest. When would another opportunity present itself? Jenny liked me, and I liked her. My chance had come. She must have thought so, too. Why else would she have sought me out alone?

Grasping her shoulders, I dragged her awkwardly to the floor. She said something I couldn't catch. Maybe she called my name. I reached for the hem of her dress. She pushed my hand away. Her body grew tense. I sympathized with her, wrestling as I was with my own insecurities, but failed to find the words to soothe her.

Again, I grabbed her dress, this time with more force, and pulled it up. She flailed about, out of passion I suppose, or perhaps nervousness. When it was over, I rolled away from her. Then I heard her sob, so I put my arms around her. We lay there for a few minutes before I spoke.

"Let's get up," I whispered. "They might start looking for you." We got to our feet. I flicked on the flashlight and tried to brush the dust from her hair and dress. She didn't speak, though she allowed me to take her hand.

By the time we reached the house, her tears had stopped. The din from the family room had quieted. The other kids must have become engrossed in the movie. She made a beeline for the bathroom, and I returned to my cleanup chores. I imagined her slipping into the darkness of the family room, thinking of me while her classmates watched some stupid movie.

Billy and his friends could hold nothing over me now. Of course, I'd be a gentleman and not name my conquest, but next year everyone would see us together at school, and they'd know. I wondered if she'd brag to her friends.

After that night, Jenny no longer ran with the same crowd on Sunday mornings. Perhaps they knew of our encounter and were jealous. Under the watchful eye of the church elders, it proved impossible to speak to her alone.

At school, I still found it awkward around the guys. I didn't want to share my experience with Jenny. It was private. I spent a solitary sophomore year waiting for Jenny to appear the following fall.

As I began my junior year, I expected Jenny to come rushing into my arms. I could see us walking hand in hand through the halls drawing looks of envy from our schoolmates. It didn't happen that way. The difference between our grades and lunch periods conspired to keep us apart.

While waiting for the bus one afternoon that first week, I found myself next to Billy Strayhorn. He had gotten into trouble and failed to graduate the previous year. While standing there, I spied Jenny getting on the adjacent bus. Billy must have noticed me watching her.

"You like that skinny bitch?" he sneered. "She's too boney to ..."

I moved swiftly away before I heard the rest. When I reached the far end of the bus zone, I turned and looked back. He was laughing and whispering to his friends, who shared his amusement.

"Morons," I muttered under my breath.

"Hey, Chris," Billy yelled across the mass of queuing students. "Your little sister and my brother ..." He didn't finish, but he made an obscene gesture, thrusting the forefinger of one hand into the fist of the other. I left the bus zone and caught a ride with Graham, whose mother always picked him up. I spent my whole junior year dodging Billy while trying to catch a glimpse of Jenny. It was hell.

Things got better in my senior year. Billy disappeared from my life. Whether he graduated, got expelled, or just dropped out, I never knew and didn't care. Best of all, my parents let me drive Mom's car occasionally.

With transportation, a cell phone, and a degree of senior swagger came dating. I called Jenny's number several times. She never answered. Her strict parents probably didn't allow her to date. However, some of the juniors and sophomores were interested enough to respond. I managed to seduce a couple of them, though they couldn't compete with my memories of Jenny.

Once, near the end of the year, I spied Jenny approaching between classes. In the crowded hallway, our eyes met. At last, I hoped to have a word with her. When I moved toward her, she turned suddenly into the restroom. The flow of students carried me past and on to my next class. I ached to make contact with her that year, but it never happened.

Upon graduating, I went off to college and majored in computer science. For a while, I tried to find Jenny on social media sites. An internet search yielded hundreds of "Jennifer McCulloughs." None were her.

During my freshman year, I hooked up several times with Sondra Jones, who I knew from high school. As the year wore on, Sondra became more focused on her studies and less on me. Other relationships followed. Only Crystal Smith lasted more than a few months. I met Crystal at a Halloween party. I went as a pirate and she as a geisha. We continued to play pirate and geisha for a semester and a half. She finally tired of the game and started dating an MBA student.

After college I took a job in the IT department of a big company in Atlanta. I found making friends in the big city difficult. I got a cat but longed for a girlfriend. As usual, the girls I conjured up looked like Jenny. I tried online dating for a while, without any great success. Eventually, I gave up and resigned myself to a solitary life.

I had been in Atlanta for two years when Betsy called on a rainy Sunday afternoon in February. She had graduated from college and moved to Seattle with her boyfriend, James—her childhood crush on Greg Strayhorn long forgotten. James was in grad school there, and Betsy had landed an office job with the phone company.

"Hey, Chris, how are you?" she chirped.

"Okay, I guess."

"I just talked to Mom and Dad a couple of days ago."

"Yeah, how are they doing?" I asked.

"They're fine, but you should give them a call

sometime." After a pause, she added, "They worry about you."

"I know. They want me to get married and produce a couple of grandchildren for them to dote over."

"Well, they just want you to find someone to be with. It's tough being alone, isn't it?"

"I've got Rosie."

"Who? Oh, right, the cat. It's not the same, Chris. We've got to get you fixed up with someone."

"Forget it. I'll worry about it when I find the right person." Her concern had begun to agitate me. "Look, I've got to go."

"Oh, wait a minute. I nearly forgot. I ran into Jenny McCullough a week ago. She's living out here."

"Uh ... really?" The news stunned me, though I found the words to follow up. "Did she ask about me?"

"Well ... no, but when I told her you were very successful in Atlanta, she sounded interested."

I desperately sought more information. "Is she married, or anything?"

"Chris, I think you still have a crush on her."

"No ... not really." I didn't want to let on how much I still wanted her. "She was cute, but kind of skinny."

"Well, she's not married. I told her I'd give her a call if you ever came to visit. We could all have dinner and talk about the good old days."

"Perhaps I can get away next month," I said, trying to keep the excitement out of my voice.

"That's kind of sudden," accused Betsy. "Are you sure you're not still nursing a crush?"

"Nonsense, I was thinking of taking some time off anyway."

After terminating the call, I experienced a wave of elation unlike anything I had felt for a long time. She hadn't married, yet. She must still have a fondness for me. Deep inside, I knew we would end up together. After our encounter at Betsy's birthday party, she must have had trouble understanding her feelings for me. That's why she never answered my calls.

I recalled a TV show about couples who broke up with their spouses or partners and reunited with their first loves. That was to be our fate—an end to being alone and a new life with the girl of my dreams. I started checking airfares.

I flew into Seattle on a damp, overcast afternoon with no chance of spotting the iconic Space Needle or the snow-capped Mount Rainier. Betsy picked me up and drove me to her apartment near the Fremont district. The flight across three time zones had tired me, so I sat down in an easy chair and dozed off.

I awoke around six o'clock, just before James arrived home. Betsy cooked a superb dinner for us. Her transformation from an obnoxious little sister to a competent adult amazed me. Afterwards, we sat in the living room and caught up with each other's lives. Eventually, I turned the conversation to my real interest.

"So," I began, "is Jenny really joining us for dinner tomorrow night?"

"Yes," replied Betsy. "I spoke with her today. She says she's looking forward to seeing you."

"Great. How does she look these days?"

"More beautiful than ever, and I think she still has a bit of a crush on you."

My dreams were coming true. She knew she had made a mistake after that first time and would not let it happen again. I slept fitfully that night, playing out possible scenarios in my mind. Every variation ended with me going home with Jenny.

Betsy took the next day off from work and showed me around the city. We visited the famous Pike Place Market and took in some of the more offbeat sights, like the Fremont Troll. The number of homeless on the streets surprised me. They were numerous in Atlanta, but nothing like Seattle. I wondered about the crime rate. By midafternoon we returned to her apartment to relax a little before the big night.

James begged off for the evening, citing a headache. I think he didn't want to hear the three of us relive old memories. Betsy and I reached the designated location—an Italian restaurant on Fourth Street at six-thirty, the appointed time. I glanced nervously over the menu while we waited for Jenny. Betsy launched into a series of recollections of our childhood. She had developed into a lively storyteller and breathed new life into the old tales.

Jenny arrived ten minutes late. She spotted us immediately in the crowded room and waved. Gone was the gangly girl of her youth. She had grown up and filled out in all the right places. She wore her hair in a short, fashionable cut. Around the restaurant, heads turned. She glided gracefully toward us wearing a lacy, red dress and matching choker ribbon. The underbite was still there, though it seemed less pronounced. I rose to meet her.

"I've been looking forward to seeing you, Chris," she said softly.

We hugged and I held the chair for her. I could hardly speak. The awkwardness of my high school days returned. I said something about the menu, and Betsy filled the space with recommendations for this dish or that. By the time the waiter withdrew, I had collected my wits.

"How have you been, Jenny?" I asked.

"Things have been good. I'm managing a local gallery. There are a lot of interesting artists in the area." She looked like a work of art to me. I wanted to ask about boyfriends, but wasn't quite sure how to bring the subject up.

Betsy once again came to the rescue. "She's doing good all right, though she'd be better if we could find her a boyfriend."

Jenny blushed. "It's okay. I'll find one when the time is right." She smiled at me. "The artists I meet are not my type. Many of them are talented, but they tend to be high maintenance."

Betsy dominated the conversation, which suited me. Living alone had dulled my conversational skills, which were not great to begin with. Betsy's stories, aided by a bottle of wine, brought laughs and helped me relax. Our mood had become quite jovial by the time the waiter brought the check.

I hurriedly produced my credit card. When Betsy objected, I dismissed her protest with a wave of my hand. "It's not so much," I said.

Jenny gave me an affectionate smile. "Thank you, Chris. I've had a lovely evening. Would you mind walking me to my car? It's only a few blocks."

"Sure," I said, with a nod.

Betsy caught my eye and mouthed "Shall I wait?" I gave a slight shake of my head, and she smiled with the satisfaction of a matchmaker.

Jenny took my arm as we strolled along. The clear, mild night brought out throngs of young people seeking their favorite bars and restaurants. Seattle seemed like a great place to live, if you've got money.

We spoke little, occasionally noting the amazing variety of food and entertainment venues available in the city. I simply enjoyed being near her, and clearly she liked being with me. I never doubted she'd take me home with her.

She had left her car in one of those underground parking decks beneath a big hotel, which occupied an entire city block. We descended in the elevator without speaking. The doors parted, and she led me to her car, parked in a distant corner. She searched in her pocketbook for the keys.

The darkness of the deck and nearness of her body summoned up a memory of that night in the tool shed. I took her in my arms and drew her close. We kissed. Her body tensed like before, but we didn't have to hurry this time. She could take me back to her apartment. We would have time together. I tightened my grip and felt the pressure of her pocketbook against my ribs. Shifting a little, I reached for it. My discomfort increased, and then pain exploded, taking my breath away. I fell against the car, grasped my side, and found a protruding knife.

I hadn't seen the assailant. Had Jenny been hurt, too? The pain increased. She reached for the knife with both hands and tried to pull it out, but it twisted. I fell to my knees and gasped. My head struck something. Dazed, I tried to rise, only to fall against the knife. Agony tore through my body. As I lay on the concrete floor, unable to move, I heard Jenny on her cell phone. I don't remember much after that.

I awoke, alone in the hospital. Eventually, a nurse stopped by to check on me. She took my vital signs and went out to get a doctor. An eternity passed before he arrived.

"You're a lucky man," said the doctor, glancing at the various monitors surrounding my bed. "It's fortunate your girlfriend kept her wits and called for an ambulance right away. You might have bled to death."

"My ... my girlfriend?" I stuttered.

"Yes, Ms. McCullough. Isn't that right?"

"Uh ... yes."

"A police officer will contact you to get your description of the mugger. Ms. McCullough wasn't able to help much in that regard. Not surprising, really. She was quite distressed by the assault."

"She's okay, isn't she?"

"She wasn't injured, but psychologically it takes time for the effects of violence to fade. Some never get over it, if the trauma is bad enough. Don't worry, your girlfriend is young. She'll be fine. Well, you get some rest, and we'll have you out of here soon."

A couple of days later, Betsy and James took me back to their apartment. I stayed for a week. Jenny didn't come to visit. When Betsy called, Jenny explained her mother was ill and she was flying home to spend some time with her.

The cops finally got around to interviewing me, but I couldn't add anything to what Jenny had told them. It happened so quickly, and it was dark. No wonder I didn't see the mugger. Jenny saved my life by calling for the ambulance. I know she loves me. Fate has kept us apart, but "Sweet Jenny" and I will be together one day. It's just a matter of time.

The Postwar Years

It's all true. Well … most of it, anyway. Stoker, Le Fanu, and the others must have had some knowledge of my kind, though they embellished certain aspects and totally fabricated others. Literary license I suppose, but their vulgar, degrading labels felt to me like the ethnic slurs that summon up such strong emotions today. You know the ones I mean.

After the April 26th surrender, General Johnston, looking splendid in his finest gray uniform, dismissed us with a speech of great eloquence. I shall never forget it. The men clapped and cheered until weariness overtook them. Most faced a long walk home, hundreds of miles for many. I was one of the lucky ones. The homestead lay only a day and a half away. I departed from camp the following morning.

The unseasonably warm day, more like July than April, soaked my clothes with sweat. Dust and pollen drifted in the languid air, sticking to my exposed face and arms. Around sunset, dark clouds moved in, promising relief. The first drops produced a cleansing joy, but before long the storm exploded with thunder and torrents of rain. I sought shelter in an old barn.

I was just stripping off my wet clothes when a blow from behind knocked me to my knees. Before I could rise, my assailant pinned my arms to my side, bit deeply into my neck, and took my blood. His grip grew stronger; I grew weaker. My consciousness slipped away and then my life.

Later, the rain stopped. A damp chill hung in the air, but I wasn't cold. The difference between what I had been and what I had become did not fill me with any great anxiety or regret. Instead, I embraced a heightened sense of self-knowledge and a serene acceptance of my new state of being.

I dressed, though my clothes were still soggy, and went out. Despite the cloud cover obscuring the moon and stars, I could see with an astonishing clarity. I reveled in this new ability, running wildly across the fields and into the woods. Speeding among the trees, I covered miles in a matter of minutes without so much as grazing a single branch.

I came across the wide path of a railroad track cutting through the woods. Far down the line the round headlight of an approaching train glimmered through the darkness. As it neared, I leapt onto the track and raced ahead of it, staying just out of the reach of its light. It was too easy. Slowing my pace, I allowed myself to be seen. The sudden scream of the whistle and the squeal of brakes ripped through the night. I dove into the weeds alongside the track, laughing as the train screeched by.

My euphoria faded, replaced by a growing restlessness. I prowled among the trees, searching for something to sate a hunger that food would not satisfy. My suddenly acute hearing amplified the soft footfalls of another creature of the night. A fox, intent on tracking a small rodent, crossed my path. He never sensed my presence. His desperate struggles were no match for my newfound strength. I bit him between his shoulders, savoring the taste of his wild blood. When I was done, I cast the carcass aside, knowing the soulless creature would not return as I had.

With my increased speed and energy, I could have easily arrived home before morning, but I tarried. Though my plan to farm the homestead vanished with my transformation, the longing for home and family remained strong. While I walked, lost deep in thought, the sky began to lighten, and the sun peeked over the horizon. Even under the fresh green canopy, the morning light produced an unsettling sensation.

I reached the edge of the woods. A field of new tobacco, just beginning to sprout, lay before me. Without the protection of trees, I became dizzy, and my head began to ache. I staggered across the field and made an awkward effort at climbing over a split rail fence, falling heavily on the other side. A tall, stately oak offered salvation, and I made for it. Its deep shade comforted me. Beyond its shadow, the landscape blurred into a washed-out whiteness. I rested there all morning. My eyes eventually adjusted to the brightness, yet my headache persisted.

By midafternoon I decided to make a push for the homestead. My speed of the previous night was greatly diminished by the light of day. I found a discarded blue cap alongside the road. Its insignia galled me, but its bill eased the effects of the sun.

I arrived at dusk. Tossing aside the repellant cap, I headed toward the house where smoke rose from the chimney. The barn still stood, and the fields were intact. It was as if the war swept by without stopping to wreak the destruction I had seen in many places. Then I noticed the tiny graveyard. Two plots, with crudely chiseled headstones, lay there. The inscriptions read "Captain Joshua T. Wilkins, C.S.A." and "Emma Mae Wilkins." Footsteps approached from behind.

"Hello, Jake. Welcome home."

I turned and hugged Billy. He buried his face against my chest and began sobbing. For long minutes, we stood there until the last light faded from the sky. Finally we separated, and he spoke in a low, sorrowful voice.

"Dad's not really there, you know. The army sent a letter. He fell at Chickamauga. After Mom died, I put up a marker for him, too. I think she would have wanted it that way. Anyway, having it there seemed right to me."

We went inside and sat at a little table, illuminated by an oil lamp. Billy offered to heat up a plate of beans.

"No thanks. I'm not hungry tonight."

"You okay, Jake? You look kinda thin. And pale, too."

"Just tired. War is ...," I began, but words failed me. I closed my eyes and took a deep breath.

"Well, I'm glad you're back." Billy exhaled a sigh of relief. "There's lots of work that needs doing around here. I'm barely getting it done by myself."

I looked him in the eye. "I can't do it. The war has changed me. My life has been unsettled. I think I'll go down to Atlanta and see what's left of it. After that ..."

"But, Jake, half the place is yours."

"No. It's all yours, Billy. I'll bet you're a better farmer now than I'll ever be."

"Stay," he pleaded. "It's too much for one person."

"You were not much more than a kid when I left. Now look at you. You've grown into a man. You can handle it. Find yourself a good woman and raise a family. You'll have the life Mom and Dad should have had if it hadn't been for that damned war."

When Billy started to respond, I raised my hand and shook my head. He gave a reluctant nod. We talked for a while of our friends and neighbors, many of whose lives had been claimed by the war. Shortly, the restless hunger began to well up inside me again. I made the excuse of going for a walk before retiring.

In the cool spring night, the exhilaration of the previous evening returned, though it was tinged with sadness. I recalled childhood memories of this home I would never see again. Beyond our cornfield, I found an ex-soldier sleeping in a makeshift tent. No doubt, he was on his own homeward journey. Pushing aside a twinge of guilt, I took what I needed, careful to leave some life in him. I had no desire to create another of my kind in Billy's backyard. That would be an unpleasant parting gift.

I stayed out all night and slept most of the next day. Billy insisted on cooking a last meal for me. I ate a little, out of politeness, though I no longer needed that kind of sustenance. After dinner I took my leave, despite Billy's concerns about the dangers of traveling at night. Departing that evening, I left the only home I had ever known. Emotions overcame me, and tears filled my eyes. It would be more than a century before I cried again.

* * *

After my transformation, it became clear my body would not age. Nineteen forever! How many times have I heard others wish for it? There were drawbacks, though. My perpetual youth would eventually attract attention. Suspicion and trouble were bound to follow, so I gravitated to large cities where I faded into the masses. I became familiar with the other denizens of the urban night—the drunkards, the addicts, the mentally ill, and sometimes the poets. Even in the company of those fringe characters, I did not linger. Always I kept moving.

For a while, I exchanged letters with Billy. He married Cynthia, a young woman from a nearby farm. They had three children, two sons and a daughter. In time, our contact grew less frequent. His last letters expressed contentment with life. When Billy died at the ripe old age of seventy, his oldest son wrote. I reflected upon his passing but experienced no deep sadness. He had lived a long, happy life. May everyone be so lucky.

When you are blessed, or cursed, with immortality, you have time to learn a lot. I took to reading. It helped to pass the lonely, interminable days and nights. Since my elusiveness allowed me to pilfer almost anything I needed or wanted, I stole books until I discovered libraries.

The 1930s were an especially memorable time for me. Lugosi's movie gave rise to popular myths, which produced absurd notions about my kind, like being able to transform into bats or wolves or having no reflection in mirrors. It was all nonsense. The advent of the social security number in 1935 made it harder for me to find the odd jobs I sometimes took to pass the time. The mass production of sunglasses turned out to be the greatest advance of the decade. I finally got some relief from the sun-induced headaches, which had plagued me for nearly seventy years.

A long existence gives you a real appreciation of history. I saw the power of the industrial revolution, the despair of the Great Depression, the chaos of two world wars, and the changes brought by the sweeping social movements of the 1960s. All in all, I wouldn't have missed any of it. When the twenty-first century rolled around, I decided it was time to return home.

* * *

The small, rural community of my youth had grown into a sizable city with a great university, both built on the economics of tobacco. I took an upstairs room in a house near campus. My landlady, Mrs. Potts, a widow in her seventies, laid down her ground rules with a strong sense of propriety. Her deceased husband had been a professor in the cultural anthropology department. I told her I worked nights.

To pay the rent, I stole. I chose my victims from the criminal class. Enormous amounts of cash could be had in a drug deal, and those hoodlums weren't about to report the theft to the police. They usually blamed each other and often destroyed themselves in the violent aftermath of suspicion and accusation. I came to think of my actions in this regard as a public service.

To sate my nightly hunger, I preyed on local church groups. They were an active bunch, with services or meetings virtually every night of the week, and their blood was less likely than that of the college kids to be awash in drugs or alcohol. I cycled through the various denominations just as we rotated crops back on the family farm, always leaving enough life so they would recuperate.

I enjoyed mingling with the students in their local night spots. These young men and women I found to be bright, quick, and engaging. They, in turn, were amazed at the depth and breadth of my accumulated knowledge. I became close with Rick, a grad student writing his dissertation on Conrad. We spent many hours dissecting the labyrinth of *Nostromo.*

And then there were the women. They, more keenly than men, sensed the power residing in me after my transformation. My sexual urges were not great, so an occasional tryst satisfied my needs. The coeds provided enough opportunities, though I never brought them to my room. I feared the disapproval of Mrs. Potts.

* * *

On a summer afternoon about a year after my arrival, Rick and I were standing in the express checkout line of a grocery. A young, blond woman in the line turned and looked past us as if recalling a forgotten item. Her eyes met mine, and she fainted without warning. She lay on the floor at my feet among a scattered assortment of vegetables.

I knelt and took her hand. When I touched her, a physical shock coursed through my body. For a moment, all went silent. Her eyelids fluttered and slowly opened, but a glazed expression lingered.

"Back up. Give her some air." Rick's deep baritone cut through the silence. The shoppers edged backwards.

The grocery manager, in rolled-up shirtsleeves, elbowed through the knot of onlookers. He propelled his short, chubby body into a blur of self-important motion, directing his customers to another checkout line. Someone brought a chair, and we helped her into it. The manager announced he had called 911 and help would be arriving soon. He pushed us aside, muttering a few words of thanks. I felt strangely compelled to stay with her, despite the eerie sensation brought on by the encounter.

"Wait," she said as I turned to go. "Who are you? I mean ..." Her voice wavered. "You, uh ... You look like my brother."

"It's a case of mistaken identity. I have no sister." I smiled, though my breathing quickened, and I glanced toward the exit.

"I know ... I mean my brother's dead, but you sure look like ... I thought you were him ... for a second. What's your name?" Out of the corner of my eye, I saw Rick at the next register paying for the groceries.

"Jake. Jake Wilkins." I started to edge away, but she followed up.

"Wilkins ... There were some Wilkinses on my father's side. We must be related."

"Not likely. I'm from Atlanta," I lied, now desperate to escape. "I've only been here a year or so." She tilted her head and rubbed the back of her neck. "Get some rest," I advised. "You'll feel better tomorrow."

Rick finally approached and nudged me. I slipped on my sunglasses, and we left. I sensed her eyes following us through the door.

Rick gave me a friendly shove. "Powerful effect you have on women. They literally fall at your feet, don't they?"

"I get no complaints," I replied with my best male bravado.

A couple of days passed, and she continued to occupy my thoughts. It wasn't that she was beautiful. Her features were rather plain, though she did have the slender body that passed for a measure of sex appeal in the twenty-first century. I preferred women with more curves.

In my heart, I knew she was family. I had lost track of Billy's sons and daughter after he died. Some of his descendants probably still resided in the area. I didn't expect to run into any of them. What were the odds? And I never considered that a family resemblance might persist for nearly a hundred and fifty years. Unable to banish the young woman from my mind, I returned to the grocery and spoke to the manager, inquiring about her health.

"She's been pestering me about you." He rubbed his bald head as he spoke. "Thinks you practically saved her life. I told her I didn't know anything about you. If you want to jot down your phone number, I'll try to remember to give it to her next time she's here." I declined, having no phone of my own, and I certainly didn't want to leave Mrs. Potts's number.

For the next week, I loitered around the area, hoping to bump into her, eventually spotting her exiting a drugstore. Still unsure of how to approach her, I followed closely while remaining unseen, a skill I had thoroughly mastered.

She passed through poor, trash-ridden neighborhoods whose population was mostly black, though whites and Latinos were present as well. It was remarkable to me how much the races mixed now, however divisions were still apparent. The war, which had been fought so fiercely a hundred and fifty years ago, seemed like a waste, rather than a noble struggle for what appeared at the time to be a principled cause. I once thought of history as a stable, unchanging thing. Now, I understand that it is in constant flux from one generation to the next.

The young woman resided in a block that had fared better than most. It was free of litter, though some of the houses were in need of repair. She lived in the back half of a brick duplex. When she entered, I heard a male voice call out a greeting. I turned away with some satisfaction in learning where she lived but disappointed by the presence of a boyfriend, or possibly a husband.

Jealousy wheedled its way into my heart, yet I knew virtually nothing about her, not even her name. The war and my transformation had robbed me of the teenage libido that grows stronger in each generation, but she aroused in me a physical attraction stronger than any I had ever known. My fervor, however, was mitigated with tenderness. I hoped she was happy and her relationship was a good one. Through the decades I've seen how precious true partnerships are. I put my desires aside in favor of not disrupting her life, though our paths were destined to cross again.

It happened on a late summer evening. I had just slipped off my sunglasses and was mulling over which church to visit that night. The Baptists, who were having revival services all week, seemed like a good choice.

"Hey!" She approached rapidly along the sidewalk. "I've been looking for you. I want to thank you for helping me at the grocery that day." She eyed me closely, reached out, and put her hand on my arm. "You sure look like my brother."

"I was glad to help. It was nothing really." Her presence brought a certain amount of undefined discomfort, yet at the same time I wanted to touch her. "I'm sorry to have brought up sad memories for you. How did your brother die?"

"Will had cancer. It was a slow, difficult death." She turned her head and bit her lip. After a few moments, she collected herself. "You're Jake, right? I'm Cindy," she said, making a valiant effort to sound cheerful.

"That's a lovely name." The tension in her face eased a bit.

"It's been in the family for eons."

She launched into a succession of questions about my past in an attempt to link us together. I had become good at improvising my personal history on short notice and blocked her at every turn. The specifics of her questions confirmed beyond doubt she was one of Billy's descendants, but I deemed it unwise to allow her to discover the truth. Finally, she exhausted the interrogation.

"Shoot! I was sure we were related." She made no effort to hide her disappointment, but after a couple of seconds, she brightened. "Then again, maybe it's for the best."

She dragged me to a nearby sandwich shop where she poured out her life story. Her parents had toiled in the tobacco factories. They both passed away just after she completed high school. Then her brother was diagnosed with cancer, and she cared for him until he died about a year ago. Now, in her early twenties, she attended a community college at night, working toward an accounting degree. Her student loan debt was piling up, but she had hopes of passing the CPA exam and landing a decent job. I wanted to help her, though I couldn't exactly hand over a suitcase full of stolen currency. A bank account was impossible for me without a social security number and various modern IDs.

She glanced at her watch. "I've got to go. What's your cell phone number?"

"I don't have one." She looked at me with raised eyebrows but did not pursue it.

"Okay, I wait tables at Sam's Diner on the weekends. I get off around ten."

She gave me a hug and kiss on the cheek before departing. My emotions were stirred by her vulnerability, and I admired her determination to overcome the hand life had dealt her. At the moment, however, I had my own needs. I pushed thoughts of her from my mind and went hunting for Baptists.

I often met Cindy at the diner and walked her home, always watching her travel the last block alone. She told me of her boyfriend, Dale, a mechanic prone to bouts of jealousy. His screaming fits were usually followed by a few days of amorous attention. It was a less than ideal relationship.

My affection for Cindy deepened, and I felt hers for me growing. I remember the first time I put my arm around her shoulders and the night she took my hand in hers, but when she pressed her body against mine for a kiss, I pulled away. We could have found a way to consummate our relationship, but I was reluctant, having grown accustomed to one-night stands. Besides, it would be unfair to embark on a long-term relationship without revealing my true nature. I couldn't see how to break the news to her.

I wondered if my resemblance to her brother affected her feelings for me. It disturbed me at first, but she rarely mentioned him, and in time I thought less about it. After all, I was not him.

I watched over her when she was unaware, once preventing a mugger from robbing her. I whisked her would-be assailant away and deposited him in a nearby alley, nursing a broken arm. Due to my carelessness, he managed to inflict a deep gash in my right forearm. I rolled up my sleeve, watched the flow of blood cease, and the cut begin to heal. The process never failed to fascinate me. I gave the startled thug a thoroughly evil snarl and flew down the alley faster than his eyes could follow.

Dale turned out to be a short, wiry guy with a thin moustache. I tracked him many nights, discovering that he supplemented his income by trafficking in illegal drugs. He operated on a rather small scale but hungered for bigger things. Trouble seemed only a matter of time. He would bear watching.

* * *

On the night of November 4, 2008, Rick and I stood in a bar with a throng of students watching the historic events unfolding on TV. Though I had no interest in politics, I marveled at how far African-Americans had come, but only needed to walk a few blocks to see how far they had yet to go.

After the holidays, the January weather turned bitter. The chilly temperatures drew Cindy closer than ever when I walked her home. Our conversation grew less, each finding comfort in the nearness of the other. I fought back my desire, and for a while she accepted our platonic friendship. One night while walking home from the diner, she finally made her move.

"Jake?"

"Yes?"

"I'm taking care of my friend's cat while she's visiting her folks."

"That's nice," I said. "I don't really get along with cats."

"Well … maybe you could come with me anyway. I've got the key to her apartment, and we could be together there."

Lust and panic are an odd combination, but I felt both keenly. When I tried to pull away, she held me tightly.

"Come with me," she pleaded, her face pressed against my chest. I pushed her from me. "Why?" she asked, searching my face for the response she desired. I looked away.

I had no answer. The truth would give her cause to doubt my sanity. I resisted the cowardly impulse to simply bolt from the scene.

"Don't deny your feelings." Her voiced quaked. Tears began to gather in the corners of her eyes.

What a fool I was to have inserted myself into her life. Her unhappiness was entirely my doing. I had to remove myself from her world. A quick break would be less painful than a protracted one. The right words eluded me.

"I don't understand you." She fought back her tears. "You care for me. I just know it."

It may have been wrong of me, but I shook my head. "Come," I said gently. "Let me take you home."

"You're trying to get rid of me!" Her voice was rising.

"No, Cindy, it's not that."

"What then?" Again, I had no explanation that would be credible to her.

"Go to hell!" she shouted and marched off in the direction of her apartment. I suppressed the impulse to chase after her, though I followed at a distance to see her safely home.

That night, I wept alone in my room. I almost didn't hear the timid tapping on my door. Drying my eyes, I slowly opened the door, hoping for Cindy but finding Mrs. Potts.

"Are you okay, Mr. Wilkins?"

"Uh ... yes ... I mean I'll be okay."

"Can I get you anything?"

"No thanks. I ... I just have to work out some things."

"Sounds like affairs of the heart," she mused. Something in my expression must have confirmed her guess. At that moment, I came closer to telling my story than I ever have or likely ever will. "Ah ... I see I'm right. Well, Mr. Wilkins, if you want someone to talk to, I'm right downstairs. Don't hesitate if you need me."

She took my hand and gave it a soft squeeze before withdrawing. I stood there, unable to think of anything except her kindness. Why couldn't I do as much for Cindy? What an ass I was.

Things done could not be undone. The way forward presented a dilemma. An apology might make a good start if she would even allow me to speak to her. Should I tell her everything? Would she believe me? Even if she did, how could we make a life together? She would age and I wouldn't. Then the only solution came to me—transformation. The choice would have to be hers. What her answer would be, I couldn't guess.

Two evenings later, I stood under the awning of an abandoned store while a cold rain fell through the wintry night. Across the street, wet students hurried to their classes at the community college. I recognized her pale-blue umbrella, bobbing in time with her familiar gait. Someone held the door for her to enter the main building. While I waited for her class to end, I imagined various scenarios playing out—some good, some bad.

When she exited the building a few minutes later, I was taken off guard. I used my quickness to position myself a couple of blocks ahead in her path. She advanced through the drizzle, walking rapidly under her umbrella and came to an abrupt halt about ten paces away.

"Cindy ..." I spoke softly, taking a step toward her. She stared back with weary eyes.

"Don't," she said.

"I'm sorry. I want to explain."

"There's nothing to say."

"But ..."

"Please leave, Jake. Don't make me cry again."

"Give me just a chance, Cindy. I don't deserve it, but ..."

"It's okay. It's my fault, too." She trembled slightly and looked away. "I let myself think ... I mean you never promised anything. I've been foolish."

"Let's talk this out. I have things to tell you."

"Go home, Jake. You'll catch your death in this weather. My class has been canceled. I just want to go home, too." She stepped around me and trudged off into the cold, rainy night.

I followed, watching over her as I had done so many times before. She couldn't have seen me, though I hoped she sensed my presence. I stood in the shadows while she covered the final block to her apartment.

I had just turned back when three loud pops of gun-fire shook me to my core. Several more rounds reverberated as I raced down the street, the rain stinging my face. The scene was chaotic. Three men were firing handguns at close range in the yard. Another lay unmoving on the ground. I broke Dale's neck without a second thought. The larger of the remaining pair rushed toward me, firing his weapon wildly. It was the last thing he ever did. By then the final gunman had fled.

Cindy lay in a pool of blood by the door. I sank to the ground cradling her head in my lap. I spoke to her, but her life was slipping away rapidly. With no time for thought, I sought her jugular and took her life before she bled to death from the gunshot. I threw my head back and howled with rage. Perhaps an element of lupine nature lurked within me after all.

Her transformation would take a few minutes. I left her there and picked up the scent of the escaped gunman. They all had to pay. I found him two blocks away sitting alone in the passenger seat of a pickup truck, his trembling hands laying out a line of cocaine on the dashboard. After dispatching him, I returned for Cindy. The police and ambulance had just arrived, the falling rain shimmering in their flashing lights, but she was gone. I wasn't worried. She was more than capable of taking care of herself, now.

The morning newspaper detailed a predictably lurid account of the events—a cocaine deal gone bad. Amazingly, the police correctly deduced Cindy's unexpected arrival had set off a panic among the conspirators and violence erupted. The authorities were searching for her. I knew they would never find her. I stayed for six months, hoping she would come to me, though I didn't know whether to expect love or fury.

* * *

Eventually, my restless nature stirred, as it always does. It was time to move on. Before I departed, I visited Billy's grave, which had been moved to a modern cemetery some decades ago, and finally paid my long overdue last respects. I shook hands with Rick and wished him luck on his dissertation. Mrs. Potts gave me a heartfelt hug and some advice on the nature of romance. Wherever I travel, I keep watching and waiting for Cindy, not knowing what she feels for me, but I'm certain our paths will cross again. After all, eternity is a long time.

* * *

Dear reader,
Thank you for taking the time to read my stories.
I hope you enjoyed them.
I would be grateful if you could leave
a review on Amazon. Reviews are the lifeblood
of independent authors.

About The Author

Ken Wetherington lives in Durham, North Carolina with his wife and two dogs. When not writing, he is an avid film buff and teaches film courses for the OLLI program at Duke University. His stories have appeared online in various publications, including *Ginosko Literary Journal, The Fable Online, Borrowed Solace: A Journal of Literary Ramblings,* and *Remington Review. Santa Abella and Other Stories* is his first book length collection. He may be reached through his web site:

www.kenwetherington.com

Made in the USA
Monee, IL
17 October 2020

45316684R00128